# TEACHER'S PET PUBLICATIONS

## LITPLAN TEACHER PACK
for
## The Lion, the Witch, and the Wardrobe
based on the book by
C. S. Lewis

Written by
Susan R. Woodward

© 2006 Teacher's Pet Publications
All Rights Reserved

This **LitPlan** for
*The Lion, the Witch and the Wardrobe*
has been brought to you by Teacher's Pet Publications, Inc.

Copyright Teacher's Pet Publications 2006
11504 Hammock Point
Berlin MD 21811

Only the student materials in this unit plan (such as worksheets, study questions, and tests) may be reproduced multiple times for use in the purchaser's classroom.

For any additional copyright questions,
contact Teacher's Pet Publications.

www.tpet.com

# TABLE OF CONTENTS - *The Lion, the Witch and the Wardrobe*

| | |
|---|---|
| Introduction | 5 |
| Unit Objectives | 7 |
| Reading Assignment Sheet | 8 |
| Unit Outline | 9 |
| Study Questions (Short Answer) | 13 |
| Quiz/Study Questions (Multiple Choice) | 24 |
| Pre-reading Vocabulary Worksheets | 45 |
| Lesson One (Introductory Lesson) | 65 |
| Nonfiction Assignment Sheet | 72 |
| Oral Reading Evaluation Form | 70 |
| Writing Assignment 1 | 74 |
| Writing Assignment 2 | 92 |
| Writing Assignment 3 | 94 |
| Writing Evaluation Form | 75 |
| Vocabulary Review Activities | 90 |
| WebQuest Project | 99 |
| Unit Review Activities | 106 |
| Extra Writing Assignments/Discussion ?s | 104 |
| Unit Tests | 111 |
| Unit Resource Materials | 143 |
| Vocabulary Resource Materials | 163 |

# INTRODUCTION

This LitPlan has been designed to develop students' reading, writing, thinking, and language skills through exercises and activities related to *The Lion, the Witch and the Wardrobe*. It includes twenty lessons supported by extra resource materials.

The **introductory lesson** introduces students to C.S. Lewis and his world. Students will work in teams to complete a questionnaire about the author of the Narnia Chronicles. Following the introductory activity, students are given a transition to explain how the activity relates to the book they are about to read. Following the transition, students are given the materials they will be using during the unit. At the end of the lesson, students begin the pre-reading work for the first reading assignment.

The **reading assignments** are approximately thirty pages each; some are a little shorter while others are a little longer. Students have approximately 15 minutes of pre-reading work to do prior to each reading assignment. This pre-reading work involves reviewing the study questions for the assignment and doing some vocabulary work for 10 vocabulary words they will encounter in their reading.

The **study guide questions** are fact-based questions; students can find the answers to these questions right in the text. These questions come in two formats: short answer or multiple choice. The best use of these materials is probably to use the short answer version of the questions as study guides for students (since answers will be more complete), and to use the multiple choice version for occasional quizzes.

The **vocabulary work** is intended to enrich students' vocabularies as well as to aid in the students' understanding of the book. Prior to each reading assignment, students will complete a two-part worksheet for 10 vocabulary words for each upcoming reading assignment. Part I focuses on students' use of general knowledge and contextual clues by giving the sentence in which the word appears in the text. Students are then to write down what they think the words mean based on the words' usage. Part II nails down the definitions of the words by giving students dictionary definitions of the words and having students match the words to the correct definitions based on the words' contextual usage. Students should then have an understanding of the words when they meet them in the text.

After each reading assignment, students will go back and formulate answers for the study guide questions. Discussion of these questions serves as a **review** of the most important events and ideas presented in the reading assignments.

After students complete reading the work, there is a **vocabulary review** lesson which pulls together all of the fragmented vocabulary lists from the reading assignments and gives students a review of all of the words they have studied. One of these will take the form of "Vocabulary Baseball" which will allow students to demonstrate that they not only recognize a word from its definition, but they can use it in correctly in a sentence. Students are expected to use their vocabulary words in the three writing assignments.

# UNIT OBJECTIVES - *The Lion, the Witch and the Wardrobe*

1. Through reading Lewis's *The Lion, the Witch and the Wardrobe*, students will study the themes of heroism, forgiveness, and change/coming of age.

2. Students will demonstrate their understanding of the text on four levels: factual, interpretive, critical, and personal.

3. Students will trace the development of the Pevensie children through their adventures in Narnia using "The Hero's Journey" developed by Joseph Campbell.

4. Students will be given the opportunity to practice reading aloud and silently to improve their skills in each area.

5. Students will read and write about the Blitz in London, the 9/11/2001 bombing of the World Trade Center and the Pentagon, and contemporary heroes.

6. Students will answer questions to demonstrate their knowledge and understanding of the main events and characters in *The Lion, the Witch and the Wardrobe* as they relate to the author's theme development.

7. Students will enrich their vocabularies and improve their understanding of the novel through the vocabulary lessons prepared for use in conjunction with the novel.

8. The writing assignments in this unit are geared to several purposes:
    a. To have students demonstrate their abilities to inform, to persuade, or to express their own personal ideas
        Note: Students will demonstrate ability to write effectively to <u>inform</u> by developing and organizing facts to convey information. Students will demonstrate the ability to write effectively to <u>persuade</u> by selecting and organizing relevant information, establishing an argumentative purpose, and by designing an appropriate strategy for an identified audience. Students will demonstrate the ability to write effectively to <u>express personal ideas</u> by selecting a form and its appropriate elements.
    b. To check the students' reading comprehension
    c. To make students think about the ideas presented by the novel
    d. To encourage logical thinking
    e. To provide an opportunity to practice good grammar and improve students' use of the English language.

9. Students will read aloud, report, and participate in large and small group discussions to improve their public speaking and personal interaction skills.

## READING ASSIGNMENT SHEET - *The Lion, the Witch and the Wardrobe*

| Date Assigned | Chapters Assigned | Date Completed |
|---|---|---|
| | 1-2 | |
| | 3-4 | |
| | 5-6 | |
| | 7-8 | |
| | 9-10 | |
| | 11-12 | |
| | 13-14 | |
| | 15-17 | |

UNIT OUTLINE - *The Lion, the Witch and the Wardrobe*

| 1<br><br>Introduction | 2<br><br>Review<br>C.S. Lewis<br>PVR 1-2 | 3<br>Study ? 1-2<br>PV 3-4<br>Nonfiction<br>Assignment | 4<br>R 3-4<br><br>Writing #1 | 5<br>Study ? 3-4<br>Peer Editing<br>PVR 5-6 |
|---|---|---|---|---|
| 6<br><br>Study ? 5-6<br>PVR 7-8 | 7<br>Study ? 7-8<br>Character<br>Poster<br>PVR 9-10 | 8<br><br>Study ? 9-10<br><br>PVR 11-12 | 9<br>Study? 11-12<br>Provoking<br>Question<br>PVR 13-14 | 10<br><br>Study ? 13-14<br><br>PVR 15-17 |
| 11<br>Study ? 15-17<br>Figurative<br>Language<br>Mini-lesson | 12<br><br>Hero's Journey | 13<br><br>Hero's Journey | 14<br><br>Vocab Review | 15<br><br>Writing #2 |
| 16<br>Peer Editing<br>Writing #3 | 17<br>Writing #3<br>Continued | 18<br>Extra<br>Discussion<br>Questions | 19<br>Unit Review | 20<br>Unit Test |

Key:  P = Preview Study Questions     V = Vocabulary Work     R= Read

# STUDY GUIDE QUESTIONS

# SHORT ANSWER STUDY GUIDE QUESTIONS - *The Lion, the Witch and the Wardrobe*

**Chapters 1-2:**
1. Why were the children sent to the Professor's home?
2. Which of the children was the youngest?
3. How did the children's adventure begin?
4. One room in the Professor's house was empty except for one thing. What was it?
5. Why did Lucy stay behind in this room after the others left?
6. Describe what Lucy found in the wardrobe.
7. Who did Lucy meet at the lamp-post? Describe him.
8. What did Mr. Tumnus call Lucy?
9. What did Lucy do while she was in Narnia?
10. What happened to Lucy while she was at Mr. Tumnus's cave?
11. Why was Mr. Tumnus crying?
12. What did Lucy give Mr. Tumnus to keep?

**Chapters 3-4:**
1. What did the others say after Lucy told them that she'd been gone for hours and hours?
2. What did the children find when Lucy showed them the wardrobe?
3. Who made fun of Lucy about her story of the wardrobe?
4. How did Lucy end up in the wardrobe a second time?
5. Who followed Lucy into the wardrobe?
6. Describe the White Witch.
7. What did the White Witch ask Edmund about who he was?
8. What did the Witch give Edmund?
9. What did the Witch want Edmund to do?
10. Who did Edmund hear calling his name as he watched the White Witch drive off?

**Chapters 5-6:**
1. What did Edmund tell the others when Lucy announced that he had made it to Narnia, too?
2. What did Peter think was wrong with Lucy since she kept talking about the wardrobe?
3. When the Professor asked Peter and Susan which of their other siblings was the more truthful, whom did they agree was?
4. Who frequently came to the Professor's house? Why?
5. How did all four of the Pevensie children end up in the wardrobe?
6. What did the Pevensive children discover in the wardrobe?
7. What was Peter's reaction toward Edmund when he realized Edmund had lied about being in Narnia?
8. What did the children find when they went to Mr. Tumnus's cave?
9. What happened to Mr. Tumnus?

*The Lion, the Witch and the Wardrobe* Short Answer Study Question page 2

**Chapters 7-8:**
1. What did the children follow into the woods after leaving Mr. Tumnus's cave?
2. Who did the children meet in the woods?
3. Where were the children taken for safety?
4. What was the "lady" of the house doing when Mr. Beaver and the children arrived?
5. Who is said to be "on the move" in Narnia?
6. Who is Aslan?
7. Mr. Beaver said the White Witch was not human, but what?
8. What did the prophecy say about the future of Narnia?
9. Who was missing after the story of the prophecy was finished?
10. Where did Mr. Beaver believe Edmund had gone?
11. Where did the Beavers take the children?

**Chapters 9-10:**
1. Why hadn't Edmund eaten his dinner at the Beavers' home?
2. What did Edmund believe about how the White Witch would treat his brother and sisters?
3. What did Edmund say was the first thing he planned to do once he was King of Narnia?
4. What did Edmund find inside the courtyard of the Witch's castle?
5. Who was Maugrim?
6. Describe the White Witch's reaction to Edmund's arrival.
7. What did the Beavers decide to do when they discovered Edmund had probably gone to see the White Witch?
8. Who did the children and the Beavers meet after they left the Beavers' house?
9. What did Father Christmas give Peter, Susan, and Lucy?

**Chapters 11-12:**
1. What did Edmund ask the White Witch to give him?
2. What did the White Witch give Edmund to eat at her castle?
3. What did the White Witch order Maugrim to do?
4. What did the woodland animals tell the Witch about where they got the feast?
5. What did the White Witch do to the woodland animals?
6. What did Edmund notice about the White Witch's sledge and the forest as they traveled to catch his brother and sisters?
7. Who did Peter, Susan, and Lucy meet at the Stone Table?
8. Why did Aslan show Peter the castle before any of the other children?
9. While viewing Cair Paraval, what did Peter hear that caught his attention?
10. What did Maugrim do to Susan and Lucy?
11. What did Peter do to Maugrim?
12. What name did Aslan give Peter?

*The Lion, the Witch and the Wardrobe* Short Answer Study Question page 3

**Chapters 13-14:**
1. What did the Witch plan to do with Edmund?
2. What happened before the Witch could carry out her plans for Edmund?
3. How did the Witch and the Dwarf escape capture?
4. What did Aslan do with Edmund?
5. Who received safe conduct to enter Aslan's camp?
6. What did the White Witch want from Aslan's camp?
7. What did the Deep Magic demand?
8. What was Aslan's response to the Witch's demand?
9. Why didn't the White Witch leave Aslan's camp with Edmund?
10. What did Peter and Aslan plan after the White Witch left Aslan's camp?
11. Who did Susan and Lucy see when they went outside their tent that night?
12. What did Susan and Lucy do when they left their tent?
13. Describe what happened at the Stone Table.

**Chapters 15-17:**
1. Who helped Susan and Lucy undo Aslan's ropes?
2. While Susan and Lucy were walking near the Stone Table, they heard a terrible noise. What was it?
3. What did Susan and Lucy see when they returned to the Stone Table?
4. How was the Witch's spell broken?
5. Where did Aslan take the girls before returning them to their brothers?
6. What did Aslan do to free the statues?
7. Who was Lucy overjoyed to find at the Witch's castle?
8. Who or what was Rumblebuffin?
9. What did the girls find when they returned to their brothers?
10. What was Edmund's contribution to the victory?
11. What happened to the White Witch?
12. How did Lucy use her gift that had been given to her by Father Christmas?
13. Describe the event of the day after the battle.
14. What names were each of the children given?
15. Who left the celebration of the New Kings and Queens?
16. What did Mr. Beaver say about Aslan's leaving?
17. What were the four "children" doing in the forest years later?
18. What did the "children" find in the forest years later?
19. What happened once the "children" started to walk down an old, familiar path?
20. What was the Professor's advice to the children in the end?

# ANSWER KEY SHORT ANSWER STUDY GUIDE QUESTIONS
*The Lion, the Witch and the Wardrobe*

**Chapters 1-2:**

1. Why were the children sent to the Professor's home?
    *There were sent away from London during the war because of the air-raids.*

2. Which of the children was the youngest?
    *Lucy was the youngest.*

3. How did the children's adventure begin?
    *Because it was raining, the children could not go outside to explore, so Peter said he was gong to explore the house, and the other children agreed.*

4. One room in the Professor's house was empty except for one thing. What was it?
    *It was a large wardrobe; the sort that has a looking-glass in the door.*

5. Why did Lucy stay behind in this room after the others left?
    *She wanted to see what was in the wardrobe.*

6. Describe what Lucy found in the wardrobe.
    *She found the land of Narnia. She also saw snow, trees, a lamp post.*

7. Who did Lucy meet at the lamp post? Describe him.
    *She met the Faun, Mr. Tumnus, who is half goat and half man. He was carrying some packages and an umbrella, and he wore a red muffler around his neck.*

8. What did Mr. Tumnus call Lucy?
    *Mr. Tumnus called Lucy a Daughter of Eve.*

9. What did Lucy do while she was in Narnia?
    *She went to Mr. Tumnus's cave for tea.*

10. What happened to Lucy while she was at Mr. Tumnus's cave?
    *Mr. Tumnus lulled her to sleep with his flute.*

11. Why was Mr. Tumnus crying?
    *He did not want to turn Lucy over to the White Witch, but he had taken service under her and was afraid of what she would do if he did not turn a Daughter of Eve over to her, as he had been instructed to do.*

12. What did Lucy give Mr. Tumnus to keep?
    *She gave him her handkerchief that he'd used to dry his tears.*

*The Lion, the Witch and the Wardrobe* Short Answer Study Question Key page 2

**Chapters 3-4:**

1. What did the others say after Lucy told them that she'd been gone for hours and hours?
   *They said she'd only been in the room a few moments.*

2. What did the children find when Lucy showed them the wardrobe?
   *They found fur coats in an ordinary wardrobe.*

3. Who made fun of Lucy about her story of the wardrobe?
   *Edmund made fun of her.*

4. How did Lucy end up in the wardrobe a second time?
   *While playing hide and seek Lucy went to have one more look into the wardrobe and then hide somewhere else. But she heard footsteps and jumped in to the wardrobe.*

5. Who followed Lucy into the wardrobe?
   *Edmund followed Lucy.*

6. Describe the White Witch.
   *She was a tall lady covered in white fur up to her throat, holding a long golden wand in her right hand and wearing a golden crown. Her face was as pale as snow except for her very red mouth.*

7. What did the White Witch ask Edmund about who he was?
   *She asked if he was a human, a Son of Adam.*

8. What did the Witch give Edmund?
   *She gave him a hot drink and a large box of Turkish Delight.*

9. What did the Witch want Edmund to do?
   *She wanted Edmund to bring his brother and sisters to her house.*

10. Who did Edmund hear calling his name as he watched the White Witch drive off?
    *He heard Lucy.*

**Chapters 5-6:**

1. What did Edmund tell the others when Lucy announced that he had made it to Narnia, too?
   *He said that he and Lucy had been pretending and that there is no Narnia.*

*The Lion, the Witch and the Wardrobe* Short Answer Study Question Key page 3

2. What did Peter think was wrong with Lucy since she kept talking about the wardrobe?
   *Peter thought that Lucy was either going mad or becoming a liar.*

3. When the Professor asked Peter and Susan which of their other siblings was the more truthful, whom did they agree was?
   *They admitted that Lucy was more truthful than Edmund.*

4. Who frequently came to the Professor's house? Why?
   *Tourists often came to view the Professor's home because it is so old and beautiful.*

5. How did all four of the Pevensie children end up in the wardrobe?
   *They were trying to avoid being seen by the tour group, and since they heard noises right outside the door, they all hid in the wardrobe.*

6. What did the Pevensie children discover in the wardrobe?
   *They found themselves in Narnia.*

7. What was Peter's reaction toward Edmund when he realized Edmund had lied about being in Narnia?
   *Peter became angry with Edmund.*

8. What did the children find when they went to Mr. Tumnus's cave?
   *The cave door was broken down, and the inside was torn apart.*

9. What happened to Mr. Tumnus?
   *He was arrested by the White Witch for treason and fraternizing with humans.*

**Chapters 7-8:**

1. What did the children follow into the woods after leaving Mr. Tumnus's cave?
   *They followed a robin from tree to tree.*

2. Who did the children meet in the woods?
   *They met a beaver.*

3. Where were the children taken for safety?
   *Mr. Beaver took them to his dam.*

4. What was the "lady" of the house doing when Mr. Beaver and the children arrived?
   *Mrs. Beaver was working at her sewing machine when they arrived.*

*The Lion, the Witch and the Wardrobe* Short Answer Study Question Key page 4

5. Who is said to be "on the move" in Narnia?
   *Aslan was said to be "on the move."*

6. Who was Aslan?
   *Aslan was the true King of Narnia, who returned to save his country.*

7. Mr. Beaver said that the White Witch was not human, but what?
   *She was half Jinn and half giantess.*

8. What did the prophecy say about the future of Narnia?
   *It said that when two Daughters of Eve and two Sons of Adam sit on the four thrones at Cair Paravel, winter would be over and peace would return to Narnia.*

9. Who was missing after the story of the prophecy was finished?
   *Edmund was missing as Mr. Beaver's story ended.*

10. Where did Mr. Beaver believe Edmund had gone?
    *Mr. Beaver believed that Edmund had gone to the White Witch to betray them all.*

11. Where were the Beavers taking the children?
    *The beavers were taking them to meet Aslan at the Stone Table.*

**Chapters 9-10:**

1. Why hadn't Edmund eaten his dinner at the Beavers' home?
   *He kept thinking about eating Turkish Delight instead.*

2. What did Edmund believe about how the White Witch would treat his brother and sisters?
   *Although he thought that she would not be very nice to them, he did not think she would hurt them.*

3. What did Edmund say was the first thing he planned to do once he was King of Narnia?
   *He would build some decent roads.*

4. What did Edmund find inside the courtyard of the Witch's castle?
   *He found stone statues of animals and other creatures.*

5. Who was Maugrim?
   *Maugrim was the wolf who was Chief of the White Witch's Secret Police.*

6. Describe the White Witch's reaction to Edmund's arrival.
   *She was angry that he had not brought his brother and sisters.*

*The Lion, the Witch and the Wardrobe* Short Answer Study Question Key page 5

7. What did the Beavers decide to do when they discovered Edmund had probably gone to see the White Witch?
    *They decided to leave the dam right away before they could be caught.*

8. Who did the children and the Beavers meet after they left the Beavers' house?
    *They met Father Christmas.*

9. What did Father Christmas give Peter, Susan, and Lucy?
    *Peter was given a sword and a shield. Susan received a bow and arrows and a horn that would bring help when blown. Lucy received a small dagger and a bottle of healing cordial.*

## Chapters 11-12:

1. What did Edmund ask the White Witch to give him?
    *He asked for more Turkish Delight.*

2. What did the White Witch give Edmund to eat at her castle?
    *She had the dwarf give him water and stale bread.*

3. What did the White Witch order Maugrim to do?
    *She ordered him to take his swiftest wolves, got to the home of the beavers, and kill whatever they would find. If no one was there, they should go to the Stone Table and wait for her in hiding.*

4. What did the woodland animals tell the Witch about where they got the feast?
    *They said that Father Christmas had given it to them.*

5. What did the White Witch do to the woodland animals?
    *The White Witch turned them all to stone with her wand.*

6. What did Edmund notice about the White Witch's sledge and the forest as they traveled to catch his brother and sister?
    *The sledge moved slower and slower because the snow was melting. The forest was turning green and the flowers were beginning to bloom. Spring was arriving at last.*

7. Who did Peter, Susan, and Lucy meet at the Stone Table?
    *They met Aslan, the great Lion.*

*The Lion, the Witch and the Wardrobe* Short Answer Study Question Key page 6

8. Why did Aslan show Peter the castle before any of the other children?
   *Peter was the firstborn, and he would be High King of all the rest.*

9. While viewing Cair Paraval, what did Peter hear that caught his attention?
   *He heard Susan's horn blowing.*

10. What did Maugrim do to Susan and Lucy?
    *Susan and Lucy were attacked by Maugrim and the wolves.*

11. What did Peter do to Maugrim?
    *Peter fought and killed Maugrim with his sword.*

12. What name did Aslan give to Peter?
    *Aslan knighted him Sir Peter Wolf's-Bane.*

## Chapters 13-14:

1. What did the Witch plan to do with Edmund?
   *She planned to tie him to a tree and kill him.*

2. What happened before the Witch could carry out her plans for Edmund?
   *Edmund was rescued by Aslan's army.*

3. How did the Witch and the Dwarf escape capture?
   *The Witch turned herself into a boulder and the dwarf into a tree stump.*

4. What did Aslan do with Edmund?
   *Aslan talked to him in private before bringing him back to his brother and sisters, and all was forgiven.*

5. Who received safe conduct to enter Aslan's camp?
   *The White Witch received safe conduct.*

6. What did the White Witch want from Aslan's camp?
   *She demanded that Edmund be turned over to her.*

7. What did the Deep Magic demand?
   *The Deep Magic demanded that all traitors belonged to the White Witch as her lawful prey, and that for every treachery she has the right to a kill.*

8. What was Aslan's response to the Witch's demand?
   *He told everyone to stand back, and he talked with the Witch alone.*

*The Lion, the Witch and the Wardrobe* Short Answer Study Question Key page 7

9. Why didn't the White Witch leave Aslan's camp with Edmund?
   *The Witch renounced her claim on Edmund after talking with Aslan.*

10. What did Peter and Aslan plan after the Whtie Witch left the camp?
    *They planned for the upcoming battle.*

11. Who did Susan and Lucy see when they went outside their tent that night?
    *They saw Aslan slowly leaving the camp.*

12. What did Susan and Lucy do when they left their tent?
    *They followed Aslan, and then walked with him after they were discovered.*

13. Describe what happened at the Stone Table.
    *Susan and Lucy looked on from the bushes as the White Witch had Aslan tied and muzzled, shaved, and then bound to the Stone Table where she killed him with a stone knife.*

**Chapters 15-17:**

1. Who helped Susan and Lucy undo Aslan's ropes?
   *The mice gnawed the ropes.*

2. While Susan and Lucy were walking near the Stone Table, they heard a terrible noise. What was it?
   *The Stone Table cracked in two, and Aslan was gone.*

3. What did Susan and Lucy see when they returned to the Stone Table?
   *Aslan had returned to life.*

4. How was the Witch's spell broken?
   *When a willing victim who had committed no treachery was killed in the traitor's stead, the Table would crack and Death itself would start working back ward.*

5. Where did Aslan take the girls before returning them to their brothers?
   *They went to the White Witch's castle to free the captives.*

6. What did Aslan do to free the statues?
   *Aslan breathed on the statues and they returned to life.*

7. Who was Lucy overjoyed to find at the Witch's castle?
   *She found Mr. Tumnus, the Faun.*

*The Lion, the Witch and the Wardrobe* Short Answer Study Question Key page 8

8. Who or what is Rumblebuffin?
    *Rumblebuffin was a giant who had been turned to stone. He broke down the gates of the castle.*

9. What did the girls find when they returned to their brothers?
    *They were in the midst of a battle with the White Witch's army.*

10. What was Edmund's contribution to the victory?
    *Edmund broke the Witch's wand.*

11. What happened to the White Witch?
    *Aslan killed her.*

12. How did Lucy use her gift that had been given to her by Father Christmas?
    *She used the cordial to heal Edmund and the others who were hurt in the battle.*

13. Describe the event of the day after the battle.
    *The children were crowned Kings and Queens of Narnia at Cair Paravel.*

14. What names were each of the children given?
    *King Peter the Magnificent*
    *Queen Susan the Gentle*
    *King Edmund the Just*
    *Queen Lucy the Valiant*

15. Who left the celebration of the New Kings and Queens?
    *Aslan left.*

16. What did Mr. Beaver say about Aslan's leaving?
    *Mr. Beaver had warned them that Aslan would come and go because he did not like to be tied down and had other countries to attend to.*

17. What were the four "children" doing in the forest years later?
    *They were hunting a great white stag.*

18. What did the "children" find in the forest years later?
    *The found an old lamp post covered in vines.*

19. What happened once the "children" started to walk down an old, familiar path?
    *They returned to their original world, and only a moment, not years, had passed.*

20. What was the Professor's advice to the children in the end?
    *He told them not to look to get back into Narnia by the same route.*

STUDY GUIDE/QUIZ QUESTIONS - *The Lion, the Witch and the Wardrobe*
Multiple Choice Format

**Chapters 1-2:**

1. Why were the children sent to the Professor's home?
    A. They were sent there to avoid the air raids in London.
    B. They were orphaned, and the professor was their only living relative.
    C. They'd run away from home and were hiding out there.
    D. They'd been kidnapped by the Professor for ransom.

2. Which of the children was the youngest?
    A. Edmund
    B. Peter
    C. Lucy
    D. Susan

3. How did the children's adventure begin?
    A. They found a map in the Professor's office.
    B. They were trying to find a safe place to hide because of the air raids.
    C. It was raining, and they decided to explore the house.
    D. They were setting a trap for the housekeeper.

4. One room in the Professor's house was empty except for one thing. What was it?
    A. a harp
    B. a suit of armor
    C. many pictures on the walls
    D. a wardrobe

5. Why did Lucy stay behind in this room after the others left?
    A. She wanted to play the harp.
    B. She wanted to examine the suit of armor.
    C. She thought she saw the pictures move, so she wanted to study them more closely.
    D. She wanted to see what was in the wardrobe.

6. Which of the following is not one of the things Lucy found in the wardrobe?
    A. a lamp post
    B. a place filled with pine trees and snow
    C. a fur coat just her size
    D. a faun

*The Lion, the Witch and the Wardrobe* Multiple Choice Study/Quiz Questions page 2

7. Who did Lucy meet at the lamp post?
    A. The White Witch
    B. Maugrim
    C. Mr. Tumnus
    D. Mr. Beaver

8. What did Mr. Tumnus call Lucy?
    A. an inquisitive child
    B. a Daughter of Eve
    C. a human vermin
    D. a lost, mysterious creature

9. What did Lucy do while she was in Narnia?
    A. She had a feast with the woodland animals.
    B. She went to Mr. Tumnus's cave for tea.
    C. She had Turkish Delight for dinner.
    D. She had tea with Father Christmas.

10. What happened to Lucy while she was at Mr. Tumnus's cave?
    A. The White Witch gave her some candy.
    B. Aslan arrived and told Lucy to hurry home immediately.
    C. Mr. Tumnus lulled her to sleep with his flute.
    D. She pricked her finger on Mr. Tumnus's sewing machine.

11. Why was Mr. Tumnus crying?
    A. He was afraid she was hurt after pricking her finger.
    B. He did not want to turn her over to the White Witch now that he knew her.
    C. He was sorry to see her go home after just getting to know her.
    D. The White Witch punished him for trying to trick Lucy.

12. What did Lucy give Mr. Tumnus to keep?
    A. her handkerchief
    B. her sweater
    C. her locket
    D. a lock of her hair

*The Lion, the Witch and the Wardrobe* Multiple Choice Study/Quiz Questions page 3

**Chapters 3-4:**

1. What did the others say after Lucy told them that she'd been gone for hours and hours?
    A. They wondered where she had been.
    B. Peter scolded her for hiding on them.
    C. They said she'd only been in the room a few moments.
    D. Edmund told her that he wished she'd been gone for hours.

2. What did the children find when Lucy showed them the wardrobe?
    A. fur coats
    B. pine trees
    C. snow
    D. a lamp post

3. Who made fun of Lucy about her story of the wardrobe?
    A. Edmund
    B. Peter
    C. The Professor
    D. Susan

4. How did Lucy end up in the wardrobe a second time?
    A. She went back for one more look, heard foot steps, and jumped in the wardrobe.
    B. She hid in the wardrobe when playing hide and seek.
    C. She was cold and needed a warm coat to wear.
    D. She was returning a coat she'd borrowed.

5. Who followed Lucy into the wardrobe?
    A. Susan
    B. Peter
    C. Mr. Tumnus
    D. Edmund

6. What does not describe the White Witch.
    A. Pale skin
    B. Red mouth
    C. Short
    D. Wearing a golden crown

7. What did the White Witch ask Edmund about who he was?
    A. She asked if he was a Jinn, a Daughter of Eve.
    B. She asked if he was a friend or foe to Aslan.
    C. She asked if he was a human, a Son of Adam.
    D. She asked if he was a traitor to the realm.

*The Lion, the Witch and the Wardrobe* Multiple Choice Study/Quiz Questions page 4

8. What did the Witch give Edmund?
   A. Turkish Delight
   B. a handkerchief
   C. a book about Narnia history
   D. tea, cakes, and sardines

9. What did the Witch want Edmund to do?
   A. She wanted him to come to the castle for the night.
   B. She wanted him to go home and never come back to Narnia.
   C. She wanted him to bring his sisters and brother to her house.
   D. She wanted him to show her the wardrobe.

10. Who did Edmund hear calling his name as he watched the White Witch drive off?
    A. Peter
    B. Lucy
    C. Susan
    D. The Professor

*The Lion, the Witch and the Wardrobe* Multiple Choice Study/Quiz Questions page 5

**Chapters 5-6:**

1. What did Edmund tell the others when Lucy announced that he had made it to Narnia, too?
    A. He told them about meeting the Queen of Narnia.
    B. He told them that he and Lucy had only been pretending about Narnia.
    C. He told them that he met the Faun Tumnus.
    D. He told them about the great Lion, Aslan.

2. What did Peter think is wrong with Lucy since she kept talking about the wardrobe?
    A. He thought she was just trying to get attention.
    B. He thought that she spent too much time with Mr. Tumnus.
    C. He thought that she was in danger from the White Witch.
    D. He thought that she was either going mad or becoming a liar.

3. When the Professor asked Peter and Susan which of their other siblings was the more truthful, whom did they agree was?
    A. Edmund
    B. Lucy
    C. both of them
    D. neither of them

4. Who frequently came to the Professor's house? Why?
    A. The neighbors frequently came for tea.
    B. The Professor invited his students to the house for dinner.
    C. Tour groups came to see the Professor's beautiful old home.
    D. Soldiers came to sleep because the house was a safe place to stay.

5. How did all four of the Pevensie children end up in the wardrobe?
    A. They were trying not to be seen by the tourists.
    B. They were hiding from the soldiers.
    C. They were playing hide and seek, and they were looking for Lucy.
    D. Mrs. Mcready was looking for them to scold them about playing in the house.

6. What did the Pevensie children discover in the wardrobe?
    A. They found old paintings.
    B. They found Turkish Delight.
    C. They found Narnia.
    D. They found a secret entrance to the Professor's garden.

*The Lion, the Witch and the Wardrobe* Multiple Choice Study/Quiz Questions page 6

7. What was Peter's reaction toward Edmund when he realized Edmund had lied about being in Narnia?
    A. He thought it was very funny.
    B. He became very angry.
    C. He did not talk to Edmund the rest of the day.
    D. He punched Edmund in the arm.

8. What did the children find when they went to Mr. Tumnus's cave?
    A. Mr. Tumnus was not at home, but he'd left a note for Lucy to help herself to tea.
    B. The White Witch was waiting for them when they arrived.
    C. The wolves were hiding in the closets to capture the children.
    D. The door had been broken down, and the inside of the cave was destroyed.

9. What happened to Mr. Tumnus?
    A. He had gone to fetch milk and sardines for the next time Lucy came for tea.
    B. The White Witch had him arrested on charges of treason.
    C. The wolves had killed Mr. Tumnus for fraternizing with humans.
    D. Aslan had arrived and took Mr. Tumnus to safety.

*The Lion, the Witch and the Wardrobe* Multiple Choice Study/Quiz Questions page 7

**Chapters 7-8:**

1. What did the children follow into the woods right after leaving Mr. Tumnus's cave?
    A. a faun
    B. a robin
    C. a wolf
    D. a beaver

2. Who did the children meet in the woods?
    A. the White Witch
    B. Aslan
    C. a beaver
    D. Mr. Tumnus

3. Where were the children taken for safety?
    A. the beavers' dam
    B. the castle of Cair Paravel
    C. the castle of the White Witch
    D. back to Mr. Tumnus's cave

4. What was the "lady" of the house doing when Mr. Beaver and the children arrived?
    A. She was cooking dinner for them all.
    B. She was sewing on a sewing machine.
    C. She was polishing the silver.
    D. She was decorating the dam for the Christmas holiday.

5. Who was said to be "on the move" in Narnia?
    A. Edmund
    B. the White Witch
    C. the Witch's wolves
    D. Aslan

6. Who was Aslan?
    A. a traitor to Narnia
    B. an evil Jinn who claims to be the Queen of Narnia
    C. the Witch's henchmen
    D. the true King of Narnia

7. Mr. Beaver said that the White Witch was not human, but what?
    A. half Jinn and half giantess
    B. an evil Faun in disguise
    C. a she-wolf in human form
    D. snow and ice come to life

*The Lion, the Witch and the Wardrobe* Multiple Choice Study/Quiz Questions page 8

8. Which of the following is not part of the prophecy surrounding Narnia?
    A. That Narnia will forever be frozen in winter.
    B. That winter will end when Aslan returns.
    C. That peace will reign when the four thrones at Cair Paravel are rightfully filled.
    D. That Christmas will not return as long as the White Witch is in power.

9. Who was missing after the story of the prophecy was finished?
    A. Lucy
    B. Edmund
    C. Peter
    D. Susan

10. Where did Mr. Beaver believe Edmund had gone?
    A. He went to search for Mr. Tumnus.
    B. He went to see the White Witch.
    C. He went to find Aslan.
    D. He went to find the way out of Narnia.

11. Where were the Beavers taking the children?
    A. to the Stone Table to meet Aslan
    B. to Cair Paravel to sit on the thrones as kings and queens
    C. to the White Witch so that the prophecy would not be fulfilled
    D. to the wardrobe door leading back to their own world

*The Lion, the Witch and the Wardrobe* Multiple Choice Study/Quiz Questions page 9

**Chapters 9-10:**

1. Why hadn't Edmund eaten his dinner at the Beavers' home?
    A. He was too afraid to eat.
    B. He did not like fish.
    C. He kept thinking about Turkish Delight instead.
    D. He did not trust the Beavers.

2. What did Edmund believe about how the White Witch would treat his brother and sisters?
    A. She would make them King and Queens as well.
    B. She would punish them severely for not believing Edmund.
    C. She would kill them for being mean to Edmund.
    D. She might not be very nice to them, but she certainly would not hurt them.

3. What did Edmund say was the first thing he planned to do once he was King of Narnia?
    A. build some decent roads
    B. get rid of Aslan
    C. make Peter his slave
    D. eat as much Turkish delight as possible

4. What did Edmund find inside the courtyard of the Witch's castle?
    A. Peter, Susan, Lucy and the Beavers
    B. statues of animals and other creatures
    C. the White Witch's sledge
    D. Aslan turned into a statue

5. Who was Maugrim?
    A. The dwarf who works for the White Witch
    B. Mr. Beaver's real name
    C. Chief of the White Witch's Secret Police
    D. Mr. Tumnus's father

6. Describe the White Witch's reaction to Edmund's arrival.
    A. She was happy to see him.
    B. She felt sorry for him because he was hungry, so she gave him Turkish Delight.
    C. She was sad to hear the lies being told about her by the Beavers.
    D. She was angry that he had not brought his brother and sisters.

7. What did the Beavers decide to do when they discovered Edmund had probably gone to see the White Witch?
    A. take the children to meet Aslan
    B. break into the Wtich's castle to rescue Edmund
    C. hide out at Mr. Tumnus's cave
    D. hurry to Cair Paravel to make the prophecy come true

*The Lion, the Witch and the Wardrobe* Multiple Choice Study/Quiz Questions page 10

8. Who did the children and the Beavers meet after they left the Beavers' house?
   A. Maugrim
   B. The White Witch
   C. Mr. Tumnus
   D. Father Christmas

9. Which of the following are not gifts given to the children by Father Christmas?
   A. a sword and shield
   B. a dagger and a cordial
   C. a bow with arrows and a horn
   D. a crossbow and quiver

*The Lion, the Witch and the Wardrobe* Multiple Choice Study/Quiz Questions page 11

**Chapters 11-12:**

1. What did Edmund ask the White Witch to give him?
    A. warm clothes
    B. a warm drink
    C. Turkish Delight
    D. a hot meal

2. What did the White Witch give Edmund to eat at her castle?
    A. stale bread and water
    B. gruel
    C. goat's milk and Turkish Delight
    D. apples and cheese

3. What did the White Witch order Maugrim do?
    A. Kill Edmund.
    B. Go to the Beaver's dam and kill everyone they find.
    C. Go to Mr. Tumnus's cave and have him arrested.
    D. Find Aslan and destroy him.

4. What did the woodland animals tell the Witch about where they got the feast?
    A. They got it from Mr. Tumnus's cave.
    B. They got it from the Beavers, and the children that were with them.
    C. They got it from Father Christmas.
    D. They got it from the Dwarf.

5. What did the White Wtich do to the woodland animals?
    A. She tricked them into betraying the children.
    B. She turned the animal party to stone.
    C. She laughed at them and continued on her quest to find the children.
    D. She had the wolves destroy the animal party.

6. What did Edmund notice about the White Witch's sledge and the forest as they traveled to catch his brother and sisters?
    A. It was slowing down because the snow was melting.
    B. The reindeer's harnesses were wearing through.
    C. The right runner was coming loose until it could hardly move.
    D. The dwarf was taking them in the wrong direction.

7. Who did Peter, Susan, and Lucy meet at the Stone Table?
    A. Tumnus
    B. Aslan
    C. Maugrim
    D. Rumblebuffin

*The Lion, the Witch and the Wardrobe* Multiple Choice Study/Quiz Questions page 12

8. Why did Aslan show Peter the castle before any of the other children?
    A. Aslan wanted to be sure the children would like the castle.
    B. Peter was the firstborn, and he would be High King of all the rest.
    C. Lucy and Susan were tired and went to sleep.
    D. Aslan wanted to impress Peter.

9. While viewing Cari Paraval, what did Peter hear that caught his attention?
    A. He heard Lucy and Susan screaming.
    B. He heard barking and snarling.
    C. He heard a cannon fire.
    D. He heard Susan's horn blowing.

10. What did Maugrim do to Susan and Lucy?
    A. Maugrim took them to the Stone Table.
    B. Maugrim warned them the White Witch was coming.
    C. Maugrim and the wolves attacked Susan and Lucy.
    D. Maugrim hid them from Father Christmas.

11. What did Peter do to Maugrim?
    A. He put Maugrim in a cage to all to see.
    B. He fought and killed Maugrim with his sword.
    C. He drove Maugrim away from camp.
    D. He laughed at Maugrim in front of the other wolves.

12. What name did Aslan give to Peter?
    A. Peter the Great
    B. Sir Peter Wolf's-Bane
    C. Sir Peter Friend of Narnia
    D. Sir Peter Wolf Killer

*The Lion, the Witch and the Wardrobe* Multiple Choice Study/Quiz Questions page 13

**Chapters 13-14:**

1. What did the Witch plan to do with Edmund?
    A. She planned to make him King of Narnia.
    B. She planned to tie him to a tree and kill him.
    C. She planned to let him go so that she could follow him to the others.
    D. She planned to feed him to Maugrim and his wolves.

2. What happened before the Witch could carry out her plans for Edmund?
    A. He escaped from the dwarf.
    B. Aslan arrived to save the day.
    C. Aslan's army rescued Edmund.
    D. Peter arrived and saved his brother.

3. How did the Witch and the Dwarf escape capture?
    A. They rode away on the sledge.
    B. They disappeared and reappeared at the Witch's Castle.
    C. The Witch turned herself into a boulder and the dwarf into a tree stump.
    D. Maugrim and the wolves rescued them.

4. What did Aslan do with Edmund?
    A. He talked to him in private and forgave him.
    B. He confronted Edmund angrily about his treachery.
    C. He turned Edmund over to Peter to be tried as a traitor.
    D. He struck Edmund to the ground.

5. Who received safe conduct to enter Aslan's camp?
    A. Mr. Tumnus
    B. The Professor
    C. Maugrim
    D. The White Witch

6. What did the White Witch want from Aslan's camp?
    A. She wanted Aslan to kill Edmund as a traitor.
    B. She wanted Edmund to be turned over to her.
    C. She wanted to make peace with Aslan.
    D. She wanted the children to return to their own world.

7. What did the Deep Magic demand?
    A. All traitors must be turned over to the White Witch as her lawful prey.
    B. Each time the White Witch met Aslan he had to bow to her.
    C. Aslan could do anything he chose because he was king.
    D. No meeting should take place before sundown.

*The Lion, the Witch and the Wardrobe* Multiple Choice Study/Quiz Questions page 14

8. What was Aslan's response to the Witch's demand?
    A. Aslan told the Witch to leave, for she had no power in his camp.
    B. Aslan had everyone to stand back, and he talked with the Witch alone.
    C. Aslan killed the Witch.
    D. Aslan invited the Witch to tea.

9. Why didn't the White Witch leave Aslan's camp with Edmund?
    A. She renounced her claim on Edmund after talking with Aslan.
    B. Maugrim was to arrest Edmund the next day.
    C. Edmund had run away.
    D. The Witch was promised gold in exchange for Edmund.

10. What did Peter and Aslan plan after the White Witch left camp?
    A. They planned traveling arrangements for the children to return home.
    B. They planned dinner for the entire camp.
    C. They planned for battle.
    D. They planned the Witch's execution once she was captured.

11. Who did Susan and Lucy see when they went outside their tent that night?
    A. They saw Aslan slowly leaving the camp.
    B. The White Witch was entering Edmund's tent.
    C. Peter was sneaking off to find the Witch himself.
    D. Edmund was trying to escape.

12. What did Susan and Lucy do when they left their tent?
    A. They went to the water hole to get a drink.
    B. They followed Aslan and then walked with him after they were discovered.
    C. They went to Peter's tent because they were afraid.
    D. They went back to see if they could find the wardrobe.

13. What happened at the Stone Table?
    A. The White Witch and her army held a feast before the upcoming battle.
    B. The White Witch humiliated then killed Aslan.
    C. Aslan and the White Witch held a peace conference.
    D. Maugrim recited The Litany Of The Deep Magic.

*The Lion, the Witch and the Wardrobe* Multiple Choice Study/Quiz Questions page 15

**Chapters 15-17:**

1. Who helped Susan and Lucy undo Aslan's ropes?
    A. Edmund
    B. Peter
    C. some field mice
    D. Mr. Beaver

2. While Susan and Lucy were walking near the Stone Table, they heard a terrible noise. What was it?
    A. Aslan was roaring and growling in pain.
    B. The Stone Table cracked into two pieces.
    C. The White Witch's army was attacking their brothers' army.
    D. Lightening struck the ground near the Stone Table.

3. What did Susan and Lucy see when they returned to the Stone Table?
    A. Aslan had returned to life.
    B. The White Witch was hiding beneath the broken table.
    C. Maugrim had retied Aslan.
    D. Edmund was laying flowers on the broken table to honor Aslan.

4. How was the Witch's spell broken?
    A. Lucy and Susan said magic words that brought Aslan back to life.
    B. Aslan willingly gave his life for Edmund, the traitor, so the spell was broken.
    C. Edmund gave the White Witch gold to bring Aslan back to life.
    D. When Peter became a Knight he had the power to bring Aslan back to life.

5. Where did Aslan take the girls before returning them to their brothers?
    A. Cair Paravel
    B. the wardrobe
    C. Mr. Tumnus' cave
    D. the White Witch's castle

6. What did Aslan do to free the statues?
    A. Aslan killed the White Witch which automatically freed the statues.
    B. Aslan poured a cordial on them.
    C. Aslan breathed on the statues, and they returned to life.
    D. Alsan had Susan blow her horn.

7. Who was Lucy overjoyed to find at the Witch's castle?
    A. the Professor
    B. Edmund
    C. Mr. Tumnus
    D. Susan

*The Lion, the Witch and the Wardrobe* Multiple Choice Study/Quiz Questions page 16

8. Who or what was Rumblebuffin?
    A. a giant revived by Aslan
    B. the evil Jinn who fathered the White Witch
    C. Mr. Tumnus's first name
    D. the true name of the White Witch's castle and grounds

9. What did the girls find when they returned to their brothers?
    A. They found a grand feast to welcome them home.
    B. They found the brothers were in the midst of a battle with the White Witch.
    C. The White Witch had surrendered.
    D. Peter was the King of Narnia.

10. What was Edmund's contribution to the victory?
    A. He killed the White Witch.
    B. He killed the Witch's dwarf.
    C. He broke the White Witch's magic wand.
    D. He rallied the troops to victory.

11. What happened to the White Witch?
    A. She ran back to her castle.
    B. Aslan killed her.
    C. She was sent to another world.
    D. She melted when summer came.

12. How did Lucy use her gift that had been given to her by Father Christmas?
    A. She used the bow and arrow to kill a wolf that was attacking Edmund.
    B. She used the horn to call for help from Aslan's army.
    C. She used her dagger to kill the Witch's dwarf.
    D. She used the cordial to heal Edmund and the others who had been hurt in battle.

13. Describe the event of the day after the battle.
    A. The White Witch was buried.
    B. The children were crowned Kings and Queens of Narnia at Cair Paravel.
    C. The children found their way back to the wardrobe.
    D. The Professor came to Narnia to rescue the children.

14. Which name was not given to the children?
    A. King Peter the Magnificent
    B. Queen Susan the Kind
    C. King Edmund the Just
    D. Queen Lucy the Valiant

*The Lion, the Witch and the Wardrobe* Multiple Choice Study/Quiz Questions page 17

15. Who left the celebration of the new Kings and Queens?
    A. Mr. Tumnus
    B. Aslan
    C. Queen Lucy
    D. Mrs. Beaver

16. What did Mr. Beaver say about Aslan's leaving?
    A. He said Aslan did not like parties.
    B. He said Aslan had to find the White Witch's broken wand.
    C. He said Aslan would come and go because he did not like being tied down and had other countries to attend to.
    D. He said Aslan was in a hurry to get back to his other life.

17. What were the four "children" doing in the forest years later?
    A. They were trying to rebuild Narnia after the battle.
    B. They were hunting a great white stag.
    C. They were searching for the lamp post.
    D. They were out walking with Aslan.

18. What did the "children" find in the forest years later?
    A. Mr. Tumnus's cave
    B. a lamp post
    C. Turkish Delight
    D. the Beavers' dam

19. What happened once the "children" started to walk down an old, familiar path?
    A. They returned to their own world as full-grown adults.
    B. They found Mr. Tumnus's old cave and decided to fix it up for him.
    C. They found Mr. Beaver's old dam and wanted to repair it for him.
    D. They returned to their own world only moments after leaving it.

20. What was the Professor's advice to the children in the end?
    A. He told them to go back to the wardrobe anytime to go to Narnia.
    B. He told them not to believe everything they see.
    C. He told them not to look to get back into Narnia by the same route.
    D. He told them to get some sleep, because they were tired from their busy day.

# ANSWER KEY - MULTIPLE CHOICE STUDY/QUIZ QUESTIONS
## *The Lion, the Witch and the Wardrobe*

|     | Chapters 1-2 | Chapters 3-4 | Chapters 5-6 | Chapters 7-8 | Chapters 9-10 | Chapters 11-12 | Chapters 13-14 | Chapters 15-17 |
|-----|--------------|--------------|--------------|--------------|---------------|----------------|----------------|----------------|
| 1.  | A | C | B | B | C | C | B | C |
| 2.  | C | A | D | C | D | A | C | B |
| 3.  | C | A | B | A | A | B | C | A |
| 4.  | D | A | C | B | B | C | A | B |
| 5.  | D | D | A | D | C | B | D | D |
| 6.  | C | C | C | D | D | A | B | C |
| 7.  | C | C | B | A | A | B | A | C |
| 8.  | B | A | D | A | D | B | B | A |
| 9.  | B | C | B | B | D | D | A | B |
| 10. | C | B |   | B |   | C | C | C |
| 11. | B |   |   | A |   | B | A | B |
| 12. | A |   |   |   |   | B | B | D |
| 13. |   |   |   |   |   |   | B | B |
| 14. |   |   |   |   |   |   |   | B |
| 15. |   |   |   |   |   |   |   | B |
| 16. |   |   |   |   |   |   |   | C |
| 17. |   |   |   |   |   |   |   | B |
| 18. |   |   |   |   |   |   |   | B |
| 19. |   |   |   |   |   |   |   | D |
| 20. |   |   |   |   |   |   |   | C |

# PREREADING VOCABULARY WORKSHEETS

VOCABULARY CHAPTERS 1-2: *The Lion, the Witch and the Wardrobe*

Part I: Using Prior Knowledge and Contextual Clues

Below are the sentences in which the vocabulary words appear in the text. Read the sentence. Use any clues you can find in the sentence combined with your prior knowledge, and write what you think the underlined words mean on the lines provided.

1. "Did you see those mountains as we came along? And the woods! There might be eagles. There might be **stags**. There'll be hawks."

   _____

2. . . . [the] room . . . was quite empty except for one big **wardrobe**; the sort that has a looking-glass in the door.

   _____

3. . . . and they all **trooped** out again—all except Lucy.

   _____

4. Lucy felt a little frightened, but she felt very **inquisitive** and excited as well.

   _____

5. He had a red woolen **muffler** round his neck. . . .

   _____

6. . . . in the other arm he carried several brown-paper **parcels**.

   _____

7. "Ah!" said Mr. Tumnus in a rather **melancholy** voice, "if only I had worked harder at geography when I was a little faun. . . ."

   _____

8. . . . the streams would run with wine instead of water and the whole forest would give itself up to **jollification** for weeks on end.

   _____

9. "Would you believe that I am the sort of Faun to meet a poor innocent child in the wood… and invite it home to my cave, all for the sake of **lulling** it asleep. . . ?"

   _____

43

*The Lion, the Witch and the Wardrobe* Vocabulary Worksheet Chapters 1-2 Continued:

10. "Why of course I can," said Lucy, shaking him **heartily** by the hand.

_____

Part II: Determining the Meaning
    Match the vocabulary words to their dictionary definitions.

    ___ 1. stag              A. a heavy scarf worn around the neck for warmth
    ___ 2. trooped         B. a tall cabinet or closet built to hold clothes
    ___ 3. inquisitive       C. festivity; revelry
    ___ 4. muffler          D. to move or go as a group
    ___ 5. melancholy    E. something wrapped up or packaged
    ___ 6. jollification    F. sadness or depression of the spirits
    ___ 7. lulling          G. the adult male of various deer
    ___ 8. parcels         H. to cause to sleep or rest; soothe or calm
    ___ 9. wardrobe      I. with warmth and sincerity
    ___ 10. heartily       J. inclined to investigate; eager for knowledge

VOCABULARY CHAPTERS 3-4: *The Lion, the Witch and the Wardrobe*

Part I: Using Prior Knowledge and Contextual Clues

Below are the sentences in which the vocabulary words appear in the text. Read the sentence. Use any clues you can find in the sentence combined with your prior knowledge, and write what you think the underlined words mean on the lines provided.

1. "Why, you goose," said Susan . . . , "it's just an **ordinary** wardrobe, look."

2. "A jolly good **hoax**, Lu," [Peter] said as he came out again; "you have really taken us in. . . ."

3. The two elder ones did this without meaning to do it, but Edmund could be **spiteful**. . . .

4. She did not mean to hide in the wardrobe because she knew that would only set the others talking again about the whole **wretched** business.

5. . . . and at last there swept into sight a **sledge** drawn by two reindeer.

6. "And how, pray, did you come to enter my **dominions**?"

7. . . . she put a fold of her fur **mantle** around him and tucked it in well.

8. . . . instantly there appeared a round box, tied with a green silk ribbon, which, when opened, turned out to contain several pounds of the best **Turkish Delight**.

9. . . . she knew, though Edmund did not, that this was **enchanted** Turkish Delight. . . .

*The Lion, the Witch and the Wardrobe* Vocabulary Worksheet Chapters 3-4 Continued:

10. . . . Lucy . . . was too happy and excited to notice how **snappishly** Edmund spoke or how flushed and strange his face was.

_____


Part II: Determining the Meaning
   Match the vocabulary words to their dictionary definitions.

|     |                    |                                                                    |
| --- | ------------------ | ------------------------------------------------------------------ |
| ___ 1. ordinary         | A. territory of influence or control; realm                   |
| ___ 2. hoax             | B. in an irritable and short tempered manner                  |
| ___ 3. spiteful         | C. of no exceptional ability                                  |
| ___ 4. wretched         | D. a loose sleeveless coat worn over outer garments; a cloak  |
| ___ 5. sledge           | E. showing ill will and a desire to hurt                      |
| ___ 6. dominions        | F. an act intended to deceive or trick                        |
| ___ 7. mantle           | G. jellylike candy cubes covered with powdered sugar          |
| ___ 8. Turkish Delight  | H. mounted on low runners, drawn by work animals across ice   |
| ___ 9. enchanted        | I. influenced by charms or spells                             |
| ___ 10. snappishly      | J. of a poor or mean character                                |

VOCABULARY CHAPTERS 5-6: *The Lion, the Witch and the Wardrobe*

Part I: Using Prior Knowledge and Contextual Clues

Below are the sentences in which the vocabulary words appear in the text. Read the sentence. Use any clues you can find in the sentence combined with your prior knowledge, and write what you think the underlined words mean on the lines provided.

1. Up to that moment Edmund had been feeling sick, **sulky**, and annoyed with Lucy. . . .

2. . . . Edmund gave a very superior look as if he were far older than Lucy... and then a little **snigger** and said, "Oh, yes, Lucy and I have been playing. . . ."

3. "Shut up! You've been perfectly **beastly** to Lu ever since she started this nonsense about the wardrobe. . . ."

4. . . . the Professor . . . got up and found chairs for them and said he was quite at their **disposal**.

5. Peter saw to it that Edmund stopped **jeering** at [Lucy]. . . .

6. "What a filthy smell of **camphor**," said Edmund.
"I expect the pockets of these coats are full of it," said Susan, "to keep away the moths."

7. There seemed, indeed, no more to say, and presently the four **resumed** their journey.

8. The former occupant of these **premises**, the Faun Tumnus, is under arrest. . . .

9. . . . the Faun Tumnus is . . . awaiting trial on a charge of High Treason . . . and **fraternizing** with humans.

*The Lion, the Witch and the Wardrobe* Vocabulary Worksheet Chapters 5-6 Continued:

10. "I'm worried about having no food with us. I'd vote for going back and getting something from the **larder**. . . ."

_____

Part II: Determining the Meaning
   Match the vocabulary words to their dictionary definitions.

___ 1. sulky            A. to allow one to use or to be of service to another
___ 2. snigger          B. a building and its surrounding grounds
___ 3. beastly          C. a compound made of bark and leaves used to repel insects
___ 4. disposal         D. very disagreeable; unpleasant
___ 5. jeering          E. a place, such as a pantry or cellar, where food is stored
___ 6. camphor          F. to abuse vocally; to taunt
___ 7. resumed          G. a disrespectful laugh
___ 8. premises         H. to associate with others in a brotherly way
___ 9. fraternizing     I. pouting and withdrawn
___ 10. larder          J. to begin again or continue after interruption

VOCABULARY CHAPTERS 7-8: *The Lion, the Witch and the Wardrobe*

Part I: Using Prior Knowledge and Contextual Clues

Below are the sentences in which the vocabulary words appear in the text. Read the sentence. Use any clues you can find in the sentence combined with your prior knowledge, and write what you think the underlined words mean on the lines provided.

1. . . . the Beaver again popped its head out from behind the trees and **beckoned** earnestly to them.

   _____

2. . . . four trees grew so close together that their **boughs** met. . . .

   _____

3. "Not meaning to be rude, Mr. Beaver," added Peter, "but, you see, we're strangers."
   "Quite right, quite right," said the Beaver. "Here is my **token**."

   _____

4. Susan said, "What a lovely dam." And Mr. Beaver didn't say, "Hush" this time but, "Merely a **trifle** . . . And it isn't really finished!"

   _____

5. . . . trickling over . . . the dam . . . was now a glittering wall of icicles, as if the side of the dam had been covered all over with flowers and wreaths and **festoons** of the purest sugar.

   _____

6. The first thing Lucy noticed . . . was a **burring** sound, and the first thing she saw was a . . . she-beaver sitting . . . at her sewing machine.

   _____

7. ". . . you've no chance of getting into the House against her will and ever coming out alive."
   "Couldn't we use some **stratagem**?" said Peter.

   _____

8. "Couldn't we dress up as something, or pretend to be—oh, **pedlars** or anything. . .?"

   _____

*The Lion, the Witch and the Wardrobe* Vocabulary Worksheet Chapters 7-8 Continued:

9. . . . the moment I set eyes on that brother of yours I said to myself "**Treacherous**." He had the look of one who has been with the Witch and eaten her food.

_____

10. . . . she'll want to use him as a **decoy**; as bait to catch the rest of you with.

_____

Part II: Determining the Meaning
    Match the vocabulary words to their dictionary definitions.

    ___ 1. beckoned          A. a buzzing or whirring sound
    ___ 2. boughs             B. to signal or summon, as by nodding or waving
    ___ 3. token               C. something of little importance or value
    ___ 4. trifle                D. tree branches, especially large or main branches
    ___ 5. festoons           E. British word for one who travels about selling wares
    ___ 6. burring            F. something serving as proof of something else; a sign
    ___ 7. stratagem        G. something used to lure victims into danger
    ___ 8. pedlars            H. not to be relied on; not dependable or trustworthy
    ___ 9. treacherous      I. decorative garlands of flowers or leaves
    ___ 10. decoy             J. a military plan designed to deceive or surprise an enemy

VOCABULARY CHAPTERS 9-10: *The Lion, the Witch and the Wardrobe*

Part I: Using Prior Knowledge and Contextual Clues

Below are the sentences in which the vocabulary words appear in the text. Read the sentence. Use any clues you can find in the sentence combined with your prior knowledge, and write what you think the underlined words mean on the lines provided.

1. He hadn't **reckoned** on this; but he had to make the best of it.

_____

2. It seemed to be all towers; little towers with long pointed **spires** on them, sharp as needles.

_____

3. He walked on and on, past corner after corner, **turret** after turret to find the door.

_____

4. Edmund now **ventured** a little nearer, still keeping in the shadows of the arch as much as he could.

_____

5. There were stone **satyrs**, and stone wolves, and bears and foxes and cat-a-mountains of stone.

_____

6. There was a…long **lithe** creature that Edmund took to be a dragon.

_____

7. "I can't **abide** with the thought of that Witch fiddling with it," said Mrs. Beaver.

_____

8. They felt very glad, but also very **solemn**.

_____

9. When you get home, you will find your dam finished… and a new **sluice-gate** fitted.

_____

*The Lion, the Witch and the Wardrobe* Vocabulary Worksheet Chapters 1-2 Continued:

10. In this bottle . . . there is a **cordial** made of the juice of one of the fire-flowers that grow in the mountains of the sun.

_____

Part II: Determining the Meaning
   Match the vocabulary words to their dictionary definitions.

  ___ 1. reckoned        A. to put up with; tolerate
  ___ 2. spires          B. a small tower extending above a building
  ___ 3. turret          C. mythological creature composed of a man and a goat
  ___ 4. ventured        D. to rely on with confidence
  ___ 5. satyr           E. a tonic; an invigorating and stimulating medicine
  ___ 6. lithe           F. took a risk; dared
  ___ 7. abide           G. gracefully slender; moving and bending with ease
  ___ 8. solemn          H. structures that taper to a point at the top
  ___ 9. sluice-gate     I. controls the rate of water flow through a channel
  ___ 10. cordial        J. deeply earnest, serious, and sober

# VOCABULARY CHAPTERS 11-12: *The Lion, the Witch and the Wardrobe*

Part I: Using Prior Knowledge and Contextual Clues

Below are the sentences in which the vocabulary words appear in the text. Read the sentence. Use any clues you can find in the sentence combined with your prior knowledge, and write what you think the underlined words mean on the lines provided.

1. [The dwarf] grinned in a **repulsive** manner as he set [some water…and a hunk of dry bread] on the floor beside Edmund. . . .

   _____

2. . . . when the whole party saw the sledge stopping . . . , all the **gaiety** went out of their faces.

   _____

3. "What is the meaning of all this **gluttony**, this waste, this self-indulgence?"

   _____

4. Coming suddenly round a corner into a **glade** of silver birch trees, Edmund saw the ground covered in all directions with little yellow flowers. . . .

   _____

5. …wherever Edmund's eyes turned he saw birds **alighting** on branches. . . .

   _____

6. The larches and birches were covered with green, the **laburnums** with gold.

   _____

7. Mr. Beaver . . . began leading them uphill across some very deep, **springy** moss (it felt nice under their tired feet). . . .

   _____

8. The next thing they saw was a **pavilion** pitched on one side of the open place.

   _____

9. "Terrible paws," thought Lucy, "if he didn't know how to **velvet** them!"

   _____

53

*The Lion, the Witch and the Wardrobe* Vocabulary Worksheet Chapters 1-2 Continued:

10. "Rise up, Sir Peter Wolf's-**Bane**. And whatever happens, never forget to wipe your sword."

_____

Part II: Determining the Meaning
 Match the vocabulary words to their dictionary definitions.

___ 1. repulsive          A. elastic, soft, bouncy
___ 2. gaiety             B. coming down and settle, as after flight
___ 3. gluttony           C. to cover over with a soft, furry covering
___ 4. glade              D. excess in eating or drinking
___ 5. alighting          E. a tree with clusters of yellow flowers
___ 6. laburnum           F. an open space in a forest
___ 7. springy            G. an ornate tent
___ 8. pavilion           H. a state of joyful exuberance or merriment
___ 9. velvet             I. a cause of harm, ruin, or death
___ 10. bane              J. offensive or disgusting

VOCABULARY CHAPTERS 13-14: *The Lion, the Witch and the Wardrobe*

Part I: Using Prior Knowledge and Contextual Clues

Below are the sentences in which the vocabulary words appear in the text. Read the sentence. Use any clues you can find in the sentence combined with your prior knowledge, and write what you think the underlined words mean on the lines provided.

1. "How if only three were filled? That would not fulfill the **prophecy**."

   _____

2. Presently the **centaurs** and unicorns and deer and birds . . . all set off to go back to the Stone Table. . . .

   _____

3. . . . as they walked off their fur was all standing up on their backs and their tails were **bristling**.

   _____

4. "Tell you?" said the Witch, her voice going suddenly **shriller**.

   _____

5. "She has **renounced** the claim on your brother's blood."

   _____

6. Aslan explained to Peter his plan of **campaign**.

   _____

7. A howl and a **gibber** of dismay went up from the creatures when they first saw the great Lion pacing towards them. . . .

   _____

8. Four Hags, grinning and **leering**, yet also . . . hanging back and half afraid of what they had to do, had approached him.

   _____

9. For now that the first shock was over, the **shorn** face of Aslan looked to her braver, and more beautiful, and more patient than ever.

*The Lion, the Witch and the Wardrobe* Vocabulary Worksheet Chapters 1-2 Continued:

10. Then she began to **whet** her knife.

_____

Part II: Determining the Meaning
  Match the vocabulary words to their dictionary definitions.

   ___ 1. prophecy         A. a mythical being that is half man and half horse
   ___ 2. centaur          B. a prediction of the future
   ___ 3. bristling         C. to sharpen a knife
   ___ 4. shriller          D. a military operation or plan
   ___ 5. renounced      E. removed the hair or fleece from something; shaved
   ___ 6. campaign       F. high-pitched and piercing in tone or sound
   ___ 7. gibber           G. standing stiffly on end
   ___ 8. leering          H. to speak about unimportant matters rapidly
   ___ 9. shorn           I. given up, especially by formal announcement
   ___ 10. whet          J. to look with a sidelong glance with evil intent

VOCABULARY CHAPTERS 15-17: *The Lion, the Witch and the Wardrobe*

Part I: Using Prior Knowledge and Contextual Clues

Below are the sentences in which the vocabulary words appear in the text. Read the sentence. Use any clues you can find in the sentence combined with your prior knowledge, and write what you think the underlined words mean on the lines provided.

1. "It will not take us long to crush the human **vermin** and the traitors. . . ."

   _____

2. . . . the whole of that vile **rabble** came sweeping off the hill-top and down the slope. . . .

   _____

3. ". . . if she had looked a little further back, into the stillness and the darkness before Time dawned, she would have read there a different **incantation**."

   _____

4. Then he opened a great red mouth, warm and living, and gave a **prodigious** yawn.

   _____

5. "Where's that **dratted** little Witch that was running about on the ground?"

   _____

6. . . . the enemy squealed and gibbered till the wood re-echoed with the **din** of that onset.

   _____

7. At first much of their time was spent in seeking out the **remnants** of the White Witch's army and destroying them. . . .

   _____

8. And they entered into friendship and **alliance** with countries beyond the sea. . . .

   _____

9. ". . . in all my days I have never hunted a nobler **quarry**."

   _____

*The Lion, the Witch and the Wardrobe* Vocabulary Worksheet Chapters 1-2 Continued:

10. "And it seems to me we should be shamed if for any fear or **foreboding** we turned back from following so noble a beast as we now have in chase."

_____

Part II: Determining the Meaning
   Match the vocabulary words to their dictionary definitions.

   ___ 1.  vermin         A. something left over
   ___ 2.  rabble         B. a hunted animal; prey
   ___ 3.  incantation    C. words or sounds believed to have a magical effect; a spell
   ___ 4.  prodigious     D. impressively great in size or force
   ___ 5.  dratted        E. a loud harsh noise
   ___ 6.  din            F. political partnership
   ___ 7.  remnants       G. a sense of impending evil or misfortune
   ___ 8.  alliance       H. a disorderly crowd of people
   ___ 9.  quarry         I. frustrating, cursed
   ___ 10. foreboding     J. people considered hateful or highly offensive; pests

# VOCABULARY ANSWER KEY *The Lion, the Witch and the Wardrobe*

|     | Chapters 1-2 | Chapters 3-4 | Chapters 5-6 | Chapters 7-8 | Chapters 9-10 | Chapters 11-12 | Chapters 13-14 | Chapters 15-17 |
|-----|---|---|---|---|---|---|---|---|
| 1.  | G | C | I | B | D | J | B | J |
| 2.  | D | F | G | D | H | H | A | H |
| 3.  | J | E | D | F | B | D | G | C |
| 4.  | A | J | A | C | F | F | F | D |
| 5.  | F | H | F | I | C | B | I | I |
| 6.  | C | A | C | A | G | E | D | E |
| 7.  | H | D | J | J | A | A | H | A |
| 8.  | E | G | B | E | J | G | J | F |
| 9.  | B | I | H | H | I | C | E | B |
| 10. | I | B | E | G | E | I | C | G |

# DAILY LESSONS

# LESSON ONE

Objectives
1. To introduce students to the author C. S. Lewis
2. To introduce students to *The Lion, the Witch and the Wardrobe*
3. To distribute books and other related materials

Activity #1

Have students count off into five teams. Each team will be given a set of questions about author C. S. Lewis. Using the in-class resources or resources at the library/media center students will search for the answers to the questions about C. S. Lewis's life. Have each group complete the questionnaire and turn in at the end of the class.

Activity #2

Distribute the materials students will use in this unit. Explain in detail how students are to use the materials that had been given to them.

Study Guides   Students should read the study guide questions for each reading assignment prior to beginning the reading assignment to get a feeling for what events and ideas are important in the section they are about to read. After reading the section, students will (as a class or individually) answer the questions to review the important events and ideas from that section of the book. Students should keep the study guides as study materials for the unit test.

Vocabulary   Prior to reading a reading assignment, students will do vocabulary work related to the section of the book they are about to read. Following the completion of the reading of the book, there will be a vocabulary review of all the words used in the vocabulary assignments. Students should keep their vocabulary work as study materials for the unit test.

Reading Assignment Sheet   You need to fill in the reading assignment sheet to let students know by when their reading has to be completed. You can either write the assignment sheet up on a side blackboard or bulletin board and leave it there for students to see each day, or you can make copies for each student to have. In either case, you should advise students to become very familiar with the reading assignments so they know what is expected of them.

Extra Activities Center   The Unit Resource Materials portion of this LitPlan contains suggestions for an extra library of related books and articles in your classroom as well as crossword and word search puzzles. Make an extra activities center in your room where you will keep these materials for students to use. (Bring the books and articles in from the library and keep several copies of the puzzles on hand.) Explain to students that these materials are available for students to use when they finish reading assignments or other class work early.

Nonfiction Assignment Sheets (2 copies)   Explain to students that they each are to read at least two non-fiction pieces at some time during the unit (one about The Blitz on London in the 1940's and one about the 9/11/001 bombings). Students will fill out a nonfiction assignment sheet after completing each of the reading assignments to help you (the teacher) evaluate their reading experiences and to help the students think about and evaluate their own reading experiences.

<u>Books</u>  Each school has its own rules and regulations regarding student use of school books.  Advise students of the procedures that are normal for your school.

# INTRODUCTORY WORKSHEET

1. What is C. S. Lewis's full name?

2. When and where was he born?

3. Briefly describe C. S. Lewis's childhood.

4. Briefly describe C. S. Lewis's education.

5. Briefly discuss C. S. Lewis's professional career (other than as an author).

6. Name C. S. Lewis's wife and provide the date of their marriage.

7. Briefly explain who or what "The Inklings" were.

*Lion, Witch & Wardrobe* Introductory Worksheet Page 2

8. Describe at least two historical events that occurred during C. S. Lewis's life that may have had an influence upon his writing.

9. In what year was *The Lion, the Witch and the Wardrobe* first published and by what company?

10. Name at least four other full length works by C. S. Lewis and their years of publication.

# LESSON TWO

## Objective
1. To review answer sheets from C. S. Lewis research
2. To preview the study questions and vocabulary for chapters 1-2
3. To read chapters 1-2
4. To introduce Nonfiction Reading Assignment

## Activity #1

Return collected C. S. Lewis answer sheets from the previous day. Each group is to come to the front of the class and share it findings for two of the ten questions. After each group presents their answers, ask the class if they found any information they would like to add to the response given. Students can write answers on the over-head projector or board (longer responses can give important information in bulleted form.) Students should be made aware this information maybe included in the unit tests.

## Activity #2

Show students how to preview the study questions for chapters 1-2, a process they will repeat for each chapter assignment. Also, show students how to do the vocabulary pre-reading worksheets using the one for chapters 1-2 as an example. These vocabulary worksheets may be done orally with students as a whole-class activity by making a transparency for the overhead projector so all students can see the worksheet. Of course, the worksheets may also be completed individually and independently by students if you choose not to use them as a whole-class activity.

## Activity #3

Have students read Chapters 1-2 of *The Lion, the Witch and the Wardrobe* out loud in class. You probably know the best way to get readers with your class; pick students at random, ask for volunteers, or use whatever method works best for your group. If you have not yet completed an oral reading evaluation for your students this period, this would be a good opportunity to do so. A form is included with this unit for your convenience.

ORAL READING EVALUATION *The Lion, the Witch and the Wardrobe*

Name _____ Class____ Date _____

| SKILL | EXCELLENT | GOOD | AVERAGE | FAIR | POOR |
|---|---|---|---|---|---|
| Fluency | 5 | 4 | 3 | 2 | 1 |
| Clarity | 5 | 4 | 3 | 2 | 1 |
| Audibility | 5 | 4 | 3 | 2 | 1 |
| Pronunciation | 5 | 4 | 3 | 2 | 1 |
| _____ | 5 | 4 | 3 | 2 | 1 |
| _____ | 5 | 4 | 3 | 2 | 1 |

Total _____   Grade _____

Comments:

# LESSON THREE

Objective
1. To review the main ideas and events from chapter 1-2
2. To gather information about The Blitz and 9/11
3. To complete the prereading work for chapters 3-4

Activity #1
    Give students a few minutes to formulate answers for the study guide questions for chapters 1-2, and then discuss the answers to the questions in detail. Write the answers on the board or over head transparency so students can have the correct answers for study purposes.
    Note: It is a good practice in public speaking and leadership skills for individual students to take charge of leading the discussions of the study questions. Perhaps a different student could go to the front of the class and lead the discussion each day that the study questions are discussed during this unit. Of course, the teacher should guide the discussion when appropriate and be sure to fill in any gaps that students have.

Activity #2
    Using the in-class library or your library/media center resources have each student select an article about the Blitz in London during the 1940's and one about the 9/11/2001 bombings. Articles may be from magazines, books, journals, the internet, or any resource available to your students. Have the students fill out a nonfiction assignment sheet for each article. Let the students know they will be given time in the next class to work on this assignment and will need to be completed for the writing assignment in Lesson 4.

Activity #3
    When students finish their Nonfiction Reading Assignment, they should review the study questions and do the vocabulary worksheet for chapters 3-4. This assignment must be completed prior to the next class meeting.

# NONFICTION ASSIGNMENT SHEET
### (To be completed after reading the required nonfiction articles)

Name _____ Date _____

Title of Nonfiction Read _____

Written By _____ Publication Date _____

I. Factual Summary: Write a short summary of the piece you read.

II. Vocabulary
    1. With which vocabulary words in the piece did you encounter some degree of difficulty?

    2. How did you resolve your lack of understanding with these words?

III. Interpretation: What was the main point the author wanted you to get from reading his work?

IV. Criticism
    1. With which points of the piece did you agree or find easy to accept? Why?

    2. With which points of the piece did you disagree or find difficult to believe? Why?

V. Personal Response: What do you think about this piece? OR How does this piece influence your ideas?

# LESSON FOUR

<u>Objective</u>
1. To improve critical analysis and writing skills through writing an essay
2. To read chapters 3-4

<u>Activity #1</u>
    Distribute Writing Assignment # 1. Discuss the directions in detail. Give students ample tome to complete the assignment and be sure to tell them when it will bee collected.
    NOTE: Tell students if you want the peer editing done in Lesson Five as written in the lessons plans or if they are to do the peer editing as written on the assignment sheet.

<u>Activity #2</u>
    If students finish Writing Assignment 1 prior to the end of the class period, they should begin reading chapters 3-4 silently. This assignment should be completed prior to the next class period.

WRITING ASSIGNMENT 1 *The Lion, the Witch and the Wardrobe*

## PROMPT
You are reading about the Pevensie children who were removed from their London home because of Germany's Blitz on the city in the 1940's. During World War II, many families were separated as children were sent to the English countryside to escape the bombings. As a result, some family members never saw one another again. On 11 September 2001, thousands of American families were affected by the terrorist bombings of the World Trade Center in New York City, the Pentagon in Washington, D.C., and the United Airlines Flight 93 that crashed just outside Pittsburgh, Pennsylvania. Like the frightened children of the Blitz, many American children wondered about the fate of adult family members after 9/11. In these instances, childhood innocence is lost as youngsters become witnesses to the atrocities of war. Your assignment is to write an essay comparing the effects of war on families (especially as they relate to children) resulting from these events.

## PREWRITING
You have read articles about the Blitz and 9/11. Take a few moments to think about how the Blitz and 9/11 affected families and children. Make one column for the Blitz and one column for 9/11. What was the affect of the Blitz on family? Put your thoughts in the Blitz column. What was the effect of 9/11 on families? Jot your ideas in the 9/11 column. Look for similarities. Then come to a general conclusion you can make about your ideas. This will be your thesis statement.

## DRAFTING
Introduce your topic in the first paragraph, being sure to end with a thesis statement. Then write three body paragraphs, each describing a profound similarity between the effects of the Blitz and 9/11 on families. Be sure to include any appropriate quotations or information from your articles in your body paragraphs as support for your thesis. Also, incorporate at least three vocabulary words from the unit into your essay. Finally, conclude by attempting to formulate a hypothesis about why people do not seem to learn from history. End the conclusion by challenging your reader in some way.

## PEER CONFERENCE/REVISING
When you finish the draft, ask another student to look at it. You may want to give the student your worksheets and articles so he/she can double check to see you have included all the information you intended to include. After reading, he/she should tell you what is best about your essay, which parts were difficult to understand or follow, and ways in which your essay could be improved. Reread your essay considering your critic's comments and make the corrections you think are necessary.

## PROOFREADING/EDITING
Do a final proofreading of your essay, double-checking your grammar, spelling, organization, and the clarity of your ideas.

WRITING EVALUATION FORM - *The Lion, the Witch and the Wardrobe*

Name _____ Date _____

Grade _____

Circle One For Each Item:

Grammar:            correct errors noted on paper

Spelling:           correct errors noted on paper

Punctuation:        correct errors noted on paper

Legibility:         excellent      good    fair    poor

_____       excellent      good    fair    poor

_____       excellent      good    fair    poor

Strengths:

Weaknesses:

Comments/Suggestions:

## LESSON FIVE

Objectives
1. To review the main ideas and events for chapters 3-4
2. To demonstrate writing skills through peer editing and conferencing
3. To complete the prereading and reading work for chapters 5-6

Activity #1
Give students a few minutes to formulate answers for the study guide questions for chapters 3-4, and then discuss the answers to the questions in detail. Write the answers on the board or overhead projector so students can have the correct answers for study purposes.
*Note:* It is a good practice in public speaking and leadership skills for individual students to take charge of leading the discussions of the study questions. Perhaps a different student could go to the front of the class and lead the discussion each day that the study questions re discussed during the unit. Of course, the teacher should guide the discussion when appropriate and be sure to fill in any gaps the students leave.

Activity #2
Pair students and have them swap drafts of the essay completed the previous day. Have students complete a peer evaluation form for their partners and share ideas/concerns about the essays. Students will respond to their partners' critiques on the evaluation form before going back and revising their essays.

Activity #3
Tell students they have the remainder of the class period to rewrite their essays and to do the prereading and reading work for chapters 5-6. This all needs to be completed prior to the next class period.

Editor's Name _____   Date _____

Writer's Name _____   Assignment _____

# **Peer Editing for Writing Assignments**

**A. Was the topic addressed correctly?**

*If your answer is "yes," be sure to tell the writer what he/she did correctly that you especially liked. If your answer is "no," tell the writer what he/she could have included in order to write a better essay.*

*Editor:* _____
_____
_____

*Writer:* _____
_____
_____

**B. Did he/she provide enough details to support his/her answer?**

*If your answer is "yes," be sure to tell the writer what you especially liked about his/her response. If your answer is "no," you must tell the writer how he/she could improve his/her response (adding specific details that were missed, connecting to topic better, or adding embedded quotations).*

*Editor:* _____
_____
_____

*Writer:* _____
_____

**C. Identify sentence type**

*Be sure to know the difference between simple, simple with compound subject, simple with compound predicate, compound, complex, and compound-complex. Using the first body paragraph, correctly identify each sentence type. If there is sufficient sentence structure variety, tell the writer what he/she did well. If not, explain what he/she could have done differently.*

*Sentence 1:* _____   *Sentence 5:* _____

*Sentence 2:* _____   *Sentence 6:* _____

Peer Editing Worksheet Page 2

*Sentence 3:* _____   *Sentence 7:* _____

*Sentence 4:* _____   *Sentence 8:* _____

*Editor:* _____

*Writer:* _____

**D. *Address the Focus Correction Areas***
   *Did the writer follow the specifics of the essay such as (address each individually):* _____

*Organization:*

*Editor:* _____

*Writer:* _____

*Use of vocabulary words as directed:*

*Editor:* _____

*Writer:* _____

**Cite both articles:**

*Editor:* _____

*Writer:* _____

**E. *Check for errors in grammar, spelling, punctuation, etc.***

*Editor:* _____

*Writer:* _____

# LESSON SIX

<u>Objectives</u>
1. To review the main events and ideas form chapter 5-6
2. To complete the prereading work for chapters 7-8
3. To evaluate students' oral reading

<u>Activity #1</u>
Quiz - Distribute quizzes (multiple choice study/quiz questions) for Chapters 5-6 and give students about 10 minutes to complete them.
(Note: The quizzes may either be the short answer study guides or the multiple choice version.) Have students exchange papers. Grade the quizzes as a class. Collect the papers for recording the grades. (If you used the multiple choice version as a quiz, take a few minutes to discuss the answers for the short answer version if your students are using the short answer version for their study guides.)

<u>Activity #2</u>
Give students about 10 minutes or so to do the prereading work for chapters 7-8.

<u>Activity #3</u>
Continue your oral reading evaluations using chapters 7-8. If you do not finish reading in class, students should finish reading chapters 7-8 prior to your next class period.

# LESSON SEVEN

<u>Objective</u>
1. To review the main ideas and events from 7-8
2. To demonstrate understanding of characterization through the creation of character posters
3. To give the students an opportunity to practice public speaking
4. To give the students an opportunity to practice note-taking
5. To do the prereading work for chapters 9-10

<u>Activity #1</u>
Review the answers for the study questions for chapters 7-8.

<u>Activity #2</u>
Divide students into 10 pairs/groups, one for each of the following: Peter, Susan, Edmund, Lucy, Aslan, Mr. Beaver, the White Witch, Mr. Tumnus, the Professor, and Maugrim.

Each pair/group will be given a large sheet of construction paper to be used to create a character poster. On each poster, the groups must provide the following:
- the name of the character
- a labeled picture of the character based on the physical description given in the text (labels should contain page numbers as evidence)
- a list of at least three positive character traits with supporting evidence and corresponding page numbers for each
- a list of at least three negative character traits with supporting evidence and corresponding page numbers for each

\* NOTE: encourage the students to try to find SOME redeeming quality in the White Witch and Maugrim and SOMETHING not quite so positive about Aslan if possible.

<u>Activity #3</u>
After students finish their posters, each pair/group must get up in front of the class and share the information about its particular character. Those who are not presenting must take notes about the other characters. Remind students that they will all be responsible for being able to identify all of the characters on the unit test.

<u>Activity #4</u>
Remind students to complete the prereading work and read chapters 9-10 for the next class.

# LESSON EIGHT

Objectives
1. To review the main ideas and events in chapters 9-10
2. To do the prereading work for chapters 11-12
3. To give students the opportunity to practice oral reading skills

Activity #1
    Quiz - Distribute quizzes for Chapters 9-10 and give students about 10 minutes to complete them.

(Note: The quizzes may either be the short answer study guides or the multiple choice version.) Have students exchange papers. Grade the quizzes as a class. Collect the papers for recording the grades. (If you used the multiple choice version as a quiz, take a few minutes to discuss the answers for the short answer version if your students are using the short answer version for their study guides.)

Activity #2
    Give Students about 10 minutes to preview the study question and vocabulary for chapters 11-12.

Activity #3
    Read aloud chapters 11-12. If you have completed the oral reading evaluations, students may read silently.

# LESSON NINE

Objectives
1. To review the main events and ideas from chapters 11-12
2. To reflect on a thoughtful question and then write a letter
3. To demonstrate students' the ability to work silently and independently
4. To review the prereading, vocabulary work and read chapters 13-14

Activity #1
Review the study questions from chapters 11-12.

Activity #2
Pose this thought provoking question to students:
*Describe a time when you were tempted by something or someone. What did you do in this situation? Did you give in to temptation? If yes, ask yourself why you did. If not, examine what it was that kept you from giving in. Be honest with yourself.*

Have students use their responses to write a poem about the dangers of temptation using allusions to *The Lion, the Witch and the Wardrobe*.

Activity #3
After responding to the question, students should silently read chapters 13-14 and work on study guides.

## LESSON TEN

Objectives
1. To review the main ideas and events from chapters 13-14
2. To review the prereading and vocabulary work for chapters 15-17
3. To read chapters 15-17


Activity #1
 Review the study questions from chapters 13-14.

Activity #2
 Give students 10 minutes to complete the study question and vocabulary work for chapters 15-17.

Activity #3
 Have students ready Chapters 15-17 out loud. Students may read silently if the oral reading evaluations have been completed.




## LESSON ELEVEN

Objectives
1. To review the main ideas and events from chapters 15-17
2. To demonstrate the students knowledge of figurative language and the opportunity to recognize its use in *The Lion, the Witch and the Wardrobe*.

Activity #1
 Review answers to the study questions from chapters 15-17.

Activity #2
 Distribute figurative language worksheets and go over the directions. Students are to identify the type of figurative language that is used in specific examples from chapters 1-8 of Lewis' *The Lion, the Witch and the Wardrobe* and explain the significance of its use. Afterwards, students may pair up and search for further examples in chapters 9-17.

# FIGURATIVE LANGUAGE

Figurative language is speech or writing that departs from literal meaning in order to achieve a special effect or meaning, speech or writing employing figures of speech. The following figures of speech can be found in *The Lion, the Witch and the Wardrobe*.

**Idiom:** a speech form or an expression of a given language that is peculiar to itself grammatically or cannot be understood from the individual literal meanings of its elements, as in *keep tabs on;* regional speech or dialect.

**Hyperbole:** a figure of speech in which exaggeration is used for emphasis or effect

**Onomatopoeia:** the formation or use of words such as *buzz* or *murmur* that imitate the sounds associated with the objects or actions they refer to

**Allusion:** an indirect reference to a historical, mythic, or literary person, place, event, movement, etc.

**Personification:** an figure of speech where the writer describes an abstraction, a thing, or a non-human form as if it were a person

**Simile:** a comparison made with "as," "like," or "than."

**Metaphor:** a comparison between two things using a form of the verb "to be"

**Symbolism:** anything that stands for or represents something else

**Foreshadowing:** hints that the authors drops early in a work about events yet to come

# FIGURATIVE LANGUAGE WORKSHEET

For each of the following quotations from chapters 1-8 of *The Lion, the Witch and the Wardrobe*, determine the type of figurative speech that C. S. Lewis uses and explain its significance. Once you complete the worksheet, search chapters 9-17 for more examples of figurative language.

**Choose from:**

| allusion | foreshadowing | hyperbole | onomatopoeia |
| simile | symbolism | idiom | personification |

1. "We've fallen on our feet and no mistake," said Peter. "This is going to be perfectly splendid."

2. "It's about ten minutes walk from here to that dining room, and any amount of stairs and passages in between."

3. She began to walk forward, crunch, crunch over the snow and through the wood towards the other light.

4. "But I've never seen a Daughter of Eve or a Son of Adam before."

5. He told about the midnight dances and how the Nymphs who lived in the wells and the Dryads who lived in the trees came out to dance with the Fauns.

6. …old Silenus on his fat donkey would come to visit them, and sometimes Bacchus himself, and then the streams would run with wine instead of water….

7. "It's always winter and never Christmas."

8. "Why, it is she who has got all Narnia under her thumb."

9. "…I shall only be a statue of a Faun in her horrible house until the four thrones at Cair Paravel are filled – and goodness knows when that will happen, or whether it will ever happen at all."

10. "The whole wood is full of her spies. Even some of the trees are on her side."

*Lion, Witch & Wardrobe* Figurative Language Worksheet Page 2

11. "I see now you were right all along. Do come out. Make it Pax."

    _____

12. …their branching horns were gilded and shone like something on fire when the sunrise has caught them.

    _____

13. Her face was white—not merely pale, but white like snow or paper or icing-sugar, except for her very red mouth.

    _____

14. Edmund saw the drop for a second in mid-air, shining like a diamond.

    _____

15. "Sharp's the word," said Peter, and all four made off through the door at the far end of the room.

    _____

16. The coats were rather too big for them so that they came down to their heels and looked more like royal robes than coats when they had put them on.

    _____

17. …spurting through the dam there was now a glittering wall of icicles, as if the side of the dam had been covered all over with flowers and wreaths and festoons of the purest sugar.

    _____

18. "Don't you know who is the King of Beasts? Aslan is a lion—*the* Lion, the great Lion."

    _____

19. "She comes of… your father Adam's first wife, her they called Lilith. And she was one of the Jinn."

    _____

20. The snow was falling thickly and steadily, the green ice of the pool had vanished under a thick blanket.

    _____

# FIGURATIVE LANGUAGE WORKSHEET ANSWERS

1. *idiom:* Peter is saying they are lucky to have ended up at the Professor's house.

2. *hyperbole:* the dining room is probably not a ten minute walk within the house

3. *onomatopoeia:* "crunch, crunch" is the sound made my walking on the snow

4. *allusion:* Adam and Eve, according to the Bible, were the first humans; therefore, human beings could be considered as their descendants

5. *allusion:* Nymphs, Dryads, and Fauns are all creatures from mythology

6. *allusion:* Silenus and Bacchus are also mythological characters

7. *symbolism:* winter symbolizes death while Christmas (December 25, near the Winter Solstice) represents hope

8. *idiom:* it means that everything is under the White Witch's control

9. *foreshadowing:* Mr. Tumnus is turned into a statue at the Witch's court and the children fill the thrones at Cair Paravel, fulfilling the prophecy

10. *personification:* trees are given human characteristics as if they could side with the White Witch

11. *idiom:* Edmund means that he wants to make peace with Lucy

12. *simile:* the horns shining in the red sunlight are compared to something on fire

13. *simile:* it shows just how white the Witch's face is

14. *simile:* it shows how shiny the droplet of potion was; diamonds are something that are coveted, so the glittering drop might be tempting to Edmund

15. *idiom:* Peter means that they have to be careful and not get caught by the housekeeper

16. * This one has several answers:
    a. *simile:* the oversized coats are being compared to long robes that drag on the ground
    b. *foreshadowing:* the four children will later wear royal robes when they sit on the thrones at Cair Paravel
    c. *symbolism:* the "robes" symbolize their impending coronation as Kings and Queens

17. *simile:* the icicles are being compared to items made of sugar

18. *symbolism:* lions are traditionally the king of beasts, and Aslan is the true King of Narnia

19. *allusion:* refers to the myth that Adam's had a wife before Eve who became evil and was cast out of the Garden of Eden

20. *metaphor:* the snow is being compared to a blanket

# LESSON TWELVE

Objectives
1. To introduce Joseph Campbell and "The Hero's Journey"
2. To demonstrate students comprehension of the Hero's Journey pattern through analysis of the Pevensie chilren's adventures through Narnia
3. To give students the opportunity to work in cooperative groups

Activity #1

Discuss the Hero's Journey Pattern and demonstrate for students how it fits much of today's literature and movies (*Harry Potter, The Lord of the Rings, Spiderman, National Treasure,* etc.). As you go through the pattern, ask students to provide examples for each of the steps based on familiar books and movies. Have students take notes and write examples.

If you are unfamiliar with Campbell's "The Hero's Journey," go to http://www.mcli.dist.maricopa.edu/smc/journey/ref/sumary.html for information.

Activity #2

Divide students into four groups, one for each of the Pevensie children. Have each group outline the steps of the Hero's Journey for their particular character.

**Questions to keep in mind:**

What is he/she like at the beginning of the adventure? (use characterization notes)
What does he/she need to learn?
How does he/she go about learning the lesson?
Who helps him/her along the way?
Who hinders his/her progress?
What does he/she learn as a result of the journey?
How can he/she make his/her world a better place based on his/her experience?

# LESSON THIRTEEN

Objectives
1. To allow students to creatively demonstrate their understanding of The Hero's Journey through the creation of a bulletin board
2. To promote cooperative learning by having students work as a large group in the creation of the bulletin board

Activity #1
   Review the Hero's Journey pattern with students and have the group share their outlines of the adventures of the Pevensie children.

Activity #2
   Using construction paper, crayons, markers, and any other materials available for creative expression, allow students to create a bulletin board outlining the Hero's Journey of the Pevensie children (a picture of my classroom bulletin board is provided as a model. It outlines the Hero's Journey in general).

# LESSON FOURTEEN

Objective
To review all of the vocabulary work done in this unit

Activity
Choose one (or more) of the vocabulary review activities listed below and spend your class period as directed in the activity. Some of the materials for these review activities are located in the Vocabulary Resource Materials section in this LitPlan.

## VOCABULARY REVIEW ACTIVITIES

1. Divide your class into two teams and have an old-fashioned spelling or definition bee.

2. Give each of your students (or students in groups of two, three or four) a *The Lion, the Witch and the Wardrobe* Vocabulary Word Search Puzzle. The person (group) to find all of the vocabulary words in the puzzle first wins.

3. Give students a *The Lion, the Witch and the Wardrobe* Vocabulary Word Search Puzzle without the word list. The person or group to find the most vocabulary words in the puzzle wins.

4. Use a *The Lion, the Witch and the Wardrobe* Vocabulary Crossword Puzzle. Put the puzzle onto a transparency on the overhead projector (so everyone can see it), and do the puzzle together as a class.

5. Give students a *The Lion, the Witch and the Wardrobe* Vocabulary Matching Worksheet to do.

6. Divide your class into two teams. Use *The Lion, the Witch and the Wardrobe* vocabulary words with their letters jumbled as a word list. Student 1 from Team A faces off against Student 1 from Team B. You write the first jumbled word on the board. The first student (1A or 1B) to unscramble the word wins the chance for his/her team to score points. If 1A wins the jumble, go to student 2A and give him/her a definition. He/she must give you the correct spelling of the vocabulary word which fits that definition. If he/she does, Team A scores a point, and you give student 3A a definition for which you expect a correctly spelled matching vocabulary word. Continue giving Team A definitions until some team member makes an incorrect response. An incorrect response sends the game back to the jumbled-word face off, this time with students 2A and 2B. Instead of repeating giving definitions to the first few students of each team, continue with the student after the one who gave the last incorrect response on the team. For example, if Team B wins the jumbled-word face-off, and student 5B gave the last incorrect answer for Team B, you would start this round of definition questions with student 6B, and so on. The team with the most points wins!

7. Have students write a story in which they correctly use as many vocabulary words as possible. Have students read their compositions orally! Post the most original compositions on your bulletin board!

8. Divide class into two teams and play "baseball." "Pitch" definitions at students and have them use the matching word correctly in a sentence to "get a hit" and "take a base." Three strikes and he/she is out. Three outs and the next team is up.

# LESSON FIFTEEN

Objectives
1. To gather information for an essay from an auditory media (CD)
2. To use newspapers to find articles to fit a theme (heroism)
3. To compose an essay about heroism in the modern world

Activity #1
Play the song "A World Without Heroes" by Kiss. Tell students to jot down phrases about the heroes that strike them as important in the song as you play the song a second time.
NOTE: You might put a copy of the lyrics on a transparency or write the words on the board for student to see and follow as they listen.

Activity #2
Ask students to tell which phrases they thought were most important and discuss why.
Transition: Tell students that some people think there are no more real heroes today, but if we look around us we can see heroes everyday.

Activity #3
NOTE: For this activity, you need to provide newspapers or tell students to bring newspapers from home.
Distribute newspapers to each student. Explain that each student should find and cut or tear out three articles that demonstrate heroism:
    1 in your community (local news section)
    1 in your country (national news section)
    1 in the world (international news section)
For each article, students should write down what qualities of a hero the person has and how the article shows heroism.

Activity #4
Distribute Writing Assignment # 2 and discuss the directions in detail.

WRITING ASSIGNMENT 2 *The Lion, the Witch and the Wardrobe*

PROMPT
Each of the Pevensie children was heroic in his/her own way. We have discussed qualities of heroes and you have found examples of heroes in your reading. Your assignment is to persuade skeptics that our world still does have heroes.

PREWRITING
Look back at your notes about heroes – from the Hero's Journey, from the Kiss song, and from your work with the newspapers to refresh in your own mind the ideas presented.

DRAFTING
Introduce your topic (heroes still exist) in the first paragraph, being sure to end with a thesis statement. Then write four body paragraphs; one about what the world would be like without heroes, and one for each of the three articles you selected. Be sure to include embedded quotations from the song and the articles in your body paragraphs as support for your thesis. Also, incorporate at least three vocabulary words from the unit into your essay. Finally, conclude by stressing the importance of heroes and end with challenging your reader in some way.

PEER CONFERENCE/REVISING
When you finish the draft, ask another student to look at it. You may want to give the student your worksheets and articles so he/she can double check to see you have included all the information you intended to include. After reading, he/she should tell you what is best about your essay, which parts were difficult to understand or follow, and ways in which your essay could be improved. Reread your essay considering your critic's comments and make the corrections you think are necessary.

PROOFREADING/EDITING
Do a final proofreading of your essay, double-checking your grammar, spelling, organization, and the clarity of your ideas.

# LESSONS SIXTEEN AND SEVENTEEN

Objectives:
1. To read and respond to their peers' writing
2. To give and accept constructive criticism about writing and then use what they have learned to improve writing skills
3. To broaden students depth of knowledge about the characters and the book
4. To work in cooperative groups to complete character journals

Activity #1
Using a peer editing form, have students work in pairs as in lesson four to edit each other's writing assignments.

Activity #2
Students will revise and edit their writing, taking their peer's suggestions into account.

Activity # 3
Divide your class into four groups – one for each of the children. Distribute Writing Assignment #3 including the appropriate journal prompts for each group, and discuss the directions in detail.

Optional Project: If your students have computer access and time, the groups could also complete the Web Quest for their characters. The Web Quest assignment guides follow the journal prompts.

# WRITING ASSIGNMENT #3
*The Lion, The Witch, And The Wardrobe*

## PROMPT
Imagine that each of the Pevensie children kept a journal about his/her adventures through Narnia. Remember that it would be written in the first person narrative and would contain the point of view of that character in particular. Your assignment is to create a journal for the character your group has been assigned.

## PREWRITING
Meet in your group and complete the following activities:
1. Each person should independently write down 3 adjectives describing your group's character. When each person has chosen 3 adjectives, tell each other what words you have chosen and why, which should prompt a discussion of your character's traits and attitudes.
2. Read through the journal entry prompts you have been given.
3. Each group member should write a response to two of the prompts. Be sure that each question has been assigned to at least two different group members. After each person has had the opportunity to respond to two prompts, you should get together as a group and share your responses to each journal prompt, analyzing the validity of the response given regarding both the content and delivery style (choice of words, attitude, etc.)

## DRAFTING
Based on your discussions of the journal prompts written by individuals in the group, compose a written journal response to each of the prompts. You may use all or parts of responses offered by the group's members in the prewriting work; just be sure your final response is one that your character might actually write–make sure it is written in your character's voice and from your character's point of view.

## REVISING & PREPARING FOR SUBMISSION
After you complete your journal responses, make a cover for your journal. Your cover should be one like your character would make. Proofread your journal entries, make necessary corrections, and staple the final responses into the journal cover.

## NOTE:
Because this is a group writing assignment, be sure each group member proofreads the journal. If you have followed these directions properly, everyone in the group will have contributed substantially to the final product, and the grade of the final product will have been earned by all group members.

# Peter's Journal

*Write a plausible response for each of the following in Peter's voice:*

1. Peter's reaction to leaving London

2. Peter's reaction to their arrival at the Professor's home in the country

3. Peter's reaction to Lucy's wild stories

4. Peter's reaction to hearing Aslan's name for the first time

5. Peter's reaction to the gifts of the sword and shield from Father Christmas

6. Peter's reaction to killing Maugrim

7. Peter's reaction to the return of Edmund

8. Peter's reaction to his coronation as King of Narnia

9. Peter as an adult in Narnia

10. Peter's reaction to returning through the wardrobe

# Susan's Journal

*Write a plausible response for each of the following in Susan's voice:*

1. Susan's reaction to leaving London

2. Susan's reaction to their arrival at the Professor's home in the country

3. Susan's reaction to hearing Aslan's name for the first time

4. Susan's reaction to the gifts of the bow and arrows and the horn from Father Christmas

5. Susan's reaction to the return of Edmund

6. Susan's reaction to the death of Aslan

7. Susan's reaction to the resurrection of Aslan

8. Susan's reaction to her coronation as Queen of Narnia

9. Susan as an adult in Narnia

10. Susan's reaction to returning through the wardrobe

# Edmund's Journal

*Write a plausible response for each of the following in Edmund's voice:*

1. Edmund's reaction to leaving London

2. Edmund's reaction to their arrival at the Professor's home in the country

3. Edmund's reaction to Lucy's wild stories

4. Edmund's reaction to meeting the White Witch for the first time

5. Edmund's reaction to hearing Aslan's name for the first time

6. Edmund's reaction to the White Witch's anger and threats against his life

7. Edmund's reaction to his private talk with Aslan

8. Edmund's reaction after the battle

9. Edmund's reaction to his coronation as King of Narnia

10. Edmund's reaction to returning through the wardrobe

# Lucy's Journal

*Write a plausible response for each of the following in Lucy's voice:*

1. Lucy's reaction to leaving London

2. Lucy's reaction to their arrival at the Professor's home in the country

3. Lucy's reminiscing about her day with Mr. Tumnus

4. Lucy's reaction to hearing Aslan's name for the first time

5. Lucy's reaction to the gifts of the dagger and the healing cordial from Father Christmas

6. Lucy's reaction to the return of Edmund

7. Lucy's reaction to the death of Aslan

8. Lucy's reaction to her day of healing the wounded on the battlefield

9. Lucy's reaction to her coronation as Queen of Narnia

10. Lucy's reaction to returning through the wardrobe

# *The Lion, the Witch and the Wardrobe* WebQuest
## Group 1: Peter Pevensie

Welcome members of Peter Pevensie's group! You will need to collaborate on each of the following to complete your WebQuest. This project will count as one of your writing assignments.

**Part I: What's in a Name?** Upon his coronation, Peter was named "King Peter the Magnificent." In a three- body-paragraph essay, describe three examples of how Peter earned his name and why it is fitting for him. Be sure to incorporate at least six vocabulary words from the unit in your essay.

**Part II: Personalized Gifts** Father Christmas gave Peter a sword and a shield as gifts. These were not toys but tools.

> **A. The Sword:** Many characters in literature use swords as their choice of weapon. Often, the hero names his sword after a specific battle. Using the following links, research swords used in Arthurian Legend and in the Lord of the Rings trilogy. Name at least three different swords and describe how each was named. Name Peter's sword and explain why the name you have chosen is appropriate.
>
> *Lord of the Rings* swords   http://www.blades-uk.com/view_items.php?cat_id=10
> Arthurian Legend   http://www.ramsdale.org/legend.htm
>
> **B. The Shield:** Peter's shield bears the crest of Aslan. Design a crest for your own family, and make your own shield. Explain what symbols you put on it and why they represent your family.
> Heraldry on the Internet   http://digiserve.com/heraldry/

**Part III: 'Tis the Season** Using the links below, research the symbolism of the season Spring. Using textual evidence, explain how Spring relates to the growth of Peter Pevensie.
   Symbolism of Spring:   http://www.folkstory.com/articles/spring.html

http://www.traditioninaction.org/religious/f011rpSpring_Fitzgerald.htm

**Part IV: Discussion questions**
A. How might the story be different if Peter had gone into the wardrobe first?
B. What might have happened if Peter had refused to forgive Edmund?

*The Lion, the Witch and the Wardrobe* WebQuest
Group 2: Susan Pevensie

Welcome members of Susan Pevensie's group! You will need to collaborate on each of the following to complete your WebQuest.

**Part I: What's in a Name?** Upon her coronation, Susan was named "Queen Susan the Gentle." In a three- body-paragraph essay, describe three examples of how Susan earned her name and why it is fitting for her. Be sure to incorporate at least six vocabulary words from the unit in your essay.

**Part II: Personalized Gifts** Father Christmas gave Susan a bow and arrows and a horn as gifts. These were not toys but tools.
    **A. The Horn:** Many characters in mythology and literature are specifically known for their use of musical instruments. Using the following links, research Roland's horn in "The Song of Roland" and Apollo's lyre in Greek mythology. Summarize the tale surrounding these instruments and describe how each was named. Name Susan's horn explain why the name you have chosen is appropriate.
    The Lyre of Apollo   http://homepage.mac.com/cparada/GML/Apollo/html
    The Song of Roland   http://www.sacred-texts.com/neu/eng/hml/hml11.htm
    **B. The Bow and Arrows:** Arrows are often made using specific birds' feathers based on the symbolic meaning of the bird. Using the links below, research bird symbolism and select what type of bird(s) you would use to create your own arrows. Draw a picture of the bird and explain why this bird best represents you.
    Bird Symbolism          http://www.brigids-haven.com/bos/info/birds.html

**Part III: 'Tis the Season** Using the link below, research the symbolism of the season Summer. Using textual evidence, explain how Summer relates to the growth of Susan Pevensie.

The Season of Summer   http://www.serve.com/shea/germusa/midsumm.htm

**Part IV: Discussion questions**
A. How might the story have been different if Susan had gone into the wardrobe first?
B. What might have happened if Susan had not told Lucy not to tell Edmund about Aslan's sacrifice?

## *The Lion, the Witch and the Wardrobe* WebQuest
### Group 3: Edmund Pevensie

Welcome members of Edmund Pevensie's group! You will need to collaborate on each of the following to complete your WebQuest.

**Part I: What's in a Name?** Upon his coronation, Edmund was named "King Edmund the Just." In a three-body-paragraph essay, describe three examples of how Edmund earned his name and why it is fitting for him. Be sure to incorporate at least six vocabulary words from the unit in your essay.

**Part II: Personalized Gifts** Although Father Christmas did not give Edmund any gifts, he certainly received something from the White Witch!
    **A. Turkish Delight:** Edmund was tempted by the White Witch's promises of rooms full of Turkish Delight, his favorite candy. Examine the following stories of others who were faced with temptation and compare their fate with Edmund's.
    Adam and Eve: http://www.sundayschoolresources.com/bibletruths1.htm
    Pandora's Box: http://www.physics.hku.hk/~tboyce/ss/topics/prometheus.html
    **B. Promises of Grandeur:** The White Witch also tempted Edmund with promises that he would be King of Narnia one day (ironically, this turned out to be true… just not how the Witch promised it). As Edmund was leaving the beavers' dam heading for the castle of the White Witch, his chief complaint was that as soon as he was King of Narnia, the first thing he would do was to build some decent roads. Using descriptions from the novel, create a map of Narnia, outlining the roads that Edmund might have built including materials and plans that would have been needed to carry out the project.
    How a Road Gets Built: http://www.virginiadot.org/projects/pr-howroadblt.asp
    Fantasy Mapmaking: http://www.fantasymaps.com/101/

**Part III: 'Tis the Season** Using the link below, research the symbolism of the season Autumn. Using textual evidence, explain how Autumn relates to the growth of Edmund Pevensie.

Aumtumn Greetings, Customs, and Lore: http://www.mythinglinks.org/autumnequinox2000.html

**Part IV: Discussion questions**
A. How might the story have been different if Edmund had gone into the wardrobe first?
B. How might Edmund have reacted if he had not been forgiven by Aslan and the others?

## *The Lion, the Witch and the Wardrobe* WebQuest
### Group 4: Lucy Pevensie

Welcome members of Lucy Pevensie's group! You will need to collaborate on each of the following to complete your WebQuest.

**Part I: What's in a Name?** Upon her coronation, Lucy was named "Queen Lucy the Valiant." In a three-body-paragraph essay, describe three examples of how Lucy earned her name and why it is fitting for her. Be sure to incorporate at least six vocabulary words from the unit in your essay.

**Part II: Personalized Gifts** Father Christmas gave Lucy a bottle of healing cordial and a small dagger as gifts. These were not toys but tools.

> **A. The Cordial:** Many stories in mythology and literature introduce the use of healing cordials, elixirs, and vessels. Using the following links, research the Holy Grail from Arthurian Legend and in Greek mythology. Summarize the tale surrounding these instruments and describe how each was named. Name Lucy's bottle of healing cordial explain why the name you have chosen is appropriate.

King Arthur and the Holy Grail:  http://www.greatdreams.com/arthur.htm
Phial of Galandriel in *Lord of the Rings*:  http://www.tuckborough.net/objects.html#Phial of Galadriel

> **B. The Dagger:** Lucy did not use her dagger in the battle in *The Lion, the Witch and the Wardrobe*, but it was still a treasured gift from Father Christmas. Dagger hilts were often wrought with exquisite metal-work and studded with gemstones, each bearing symbols that supported the traits of its owner. Design a hilt for a dagger that could best symbolize you.

Historic Gemstone Symbolism:  http://www.jjkent.com/articles/history-symbolism-jewels.htm

**Part III: 'Tis the Season** Using the link below, research the symbolism of the season Winter. Using textual evidence, explain how Winter relates to the growth of Lucy Pevensie.

The Season of Winter  http://www.indigosun.com/Dec2000/winter_solstice.htm

**Part IV: Discussion questions**
A. How might the story have been different if Lucy had first met the Witch and not Mr. Tumnus?
B. What difference might there have been to the story if Edmund had not lied about being in the wardrobe with Lucy?

# LESSON EIGHTEEN

Objectives
    1. To widen the breadth of students' knowledge about the topics discussed or touched upon in *The Lion, the Witch and the Wardrobe*
    2. To share WebQuest

Activity #1
    Choose the questions from the Extra Discussion Questions/Writing Assignments which seem most appropriate for your students. A class discussion of these questions is most effective if students have been given the opportunity to formulate answers to the questions prior to the discussion. To this end, you may either have all the students formulate answers to all the questions, divide your class into groups and assign one or more questions to each group, or you could assign one question to each student in your class. The option you choose will make a difference in the amount of class time needed for this activity. After your students have has the opportunity to prepare responses to the questions, discuss the answers as a whole class.

Activity #2
    (Optional)WebQuest Presentations:
    If your students have completed the WebQuest, ask each student to give a brief oral report about the WebQuest projects he/she read for the unit project assignment. Your criteria for evaluating this report will vary depending on the level of your students. You may wish for students to give a complete report without using notes of any kind, or you may want students to read directly from a written report, or you may want to do something in between these two extremes. Just make students aware of your criteria in ample time for them to prepare their reports. You may need an extra class period for this activity.

    Start with one group of student's report. After that, ask if anyone else in the class has read on a topic related to the first student's report. If no one has, choose another student at random. After each report, be sure to ask if anyone has a report related to the one just completed. That will help keep continuity during the discussion of the reports. After all reports on a topic are given, take a minute to hold a short class discussion about the information students have just heard.

# EXTRA WRITING ASSIGNMENTS/DISCUSSION QUESTIONS
*The Lion, the Witch and the Wardrobe*

Interpretive
1. From what point of view is the book written, and what effect does that have on the story?
2. Is the story believable? Explain why or why not.
3. Where is the climax of the story? Explain your choice.
4. Are the characters in this book stereotypes? If so, explain the usefulness of employing stereotypes in the novel. If they are not, explain how they merit individuality.
5. What is the setting of the story? Could this story have been set in a different time and place and still have the same effect?

Critical
1. Why does Susan believe that Edmund should never be told of Aslan's sacrifice?
2. The Professor tells the children that they "won't get into Narnia again by *that* route." What does this and the fact that the Professor believed Lucy to be telling the truth right from the beginning suggest about him?
3. Explain the significance of the fact that each time the children enter Narnia it is by accident.
4. Why do you suppose C. S. Lewis mentions several times that "you should never, never shut yourself in a wardrobe"? What is significant about the one child who does not take this advice?
5. The White Witch owes much of her power to her wand, and once it is broken, her reign crumbles. Explain the significance of the fact that it was Edmund who broke the wand.
6. In ancient myths, the fertility of the land is tied to the health of a heroic figure such as a king or a knight (such as the Fisher King in Arthurian Legend). The land can be bountiful again only when a spell put on the heroic figure is broken. Explain how *The Lion, the Witch and the Wardrobe* is similar to such a myth. Then explain why the fertility of the land would be of such importance to ancient peoples.
7. Explain the irony of the children's being sent from London to avoid the effects of war only to end up being directly involved in a battle in another world. What might be suggested by Peter's and Edmund's roles in the battle?
8. Lucy uses her cordial from Father Christmas to heal the sick and wounded after the battle. Think of other healing cordials/medicines from literature and/or movies, and relate their use to Lucy's.
9. Although C. S. Lewis denied that Aslan's sacrifice in *The Lion, the Witch and the Wardrobe* is a direct allegory to the Passion of Jesus Christ, many parallels can be drawn. Compare and contrast the two events.
10. Find other elements of *The Lion, the Witch and the Wardrobe* that parallel Christianity.
11. Compare and contrast the Pevensie children's return from Narnia to Dorothy's return from Oz in *The Wonderful Wizard of Oz* by L. Frank Baum. Just because both adventures could be remembered as if only dreams, does that make the journey any less significant? Explain why or why not.

*Lion, Witch & Wardrobe Extra Discussion Questions page 2*

Critical/Personal Response
1. Suppose one of the other Pevensie children had gone into the wardrobe first. How might the story have been different if Edmund had been the first to meet Mr. Tumnus? What if Peter had been the one to meet the White Witch instead of Edmund? What if Susan was first?
2. How might the character of Edmund been different if Lucy had been allowed to tell him what Aslan had done for him?
3. What if it had been only King Peter and King Edmund hunting the stag and found the lamp post? Suppose a different ending if only the boys went back through the wardrobe and could not return to Narnia.
4. Suppose the other children had not accepted Edmund back after his betrayal. What might have been the outcome?


Personal Response
1. What was your favorite part of *The Lion, the Witch and the Wardrobe*? Why?
2. What part of the novel did you like the least? Why?
3. Would you like to read more of *The Chronicles of Narnia* by C. S. Lewis? Why or why not?
4. Which of the four Pevensie children do you most identify with? Why?

# LESSON NINETEEN

Objective
To review the main ideas and events in *The Lion, the Witch and the Wardrobe*

Activity
Choose one of the review games/activities suggested in this unit and spend your class time as directed there.

### REVIEW GAMES/ACTIVITIES *The Lion, the Witch and the Wardrobe*

1. Ask the class to make up a unit test for *The Lion, the Witch and the Wardrobe*. The test should have 4 sections: matching, true/false, short answer, and essay. Students may use 1/2 period to make the test and then swap papers and use the other 1/2 class period to take a test a classmate has devised. (open book) You may want to use the unit test included in this packet or take questions from the students' unit tests to formulate your own test.

2. Take 1/2 period for students to make up true and false questions (including the answers). Collect the papers and divide the class into two teams. Draw a big tic-tac-toe board on the chalk board. Make one team X and one team O. Ask questions to each side, giving each student one turn. If the question is answered correctly, that students' team's letter (X or O) is placed in the box. If the answer is incorrect, no letter is placed in the box. The object is to get three in a row like tic-tac-toe. You may want to keep track of the number of games won for each team.

3. Take 1/2 period for students to make up questions (true/false and short answer). Collect the questions. Divide the class into two teams. You'll alternate asking questions to individual members of teams A & B (like in a spelling bee). The question keeps going from A to B until it is correctly answered, then a new question is asked. A correct answer does not allow the team to get another question. Correct answers are +2 points; incorrect answers are -1 point.

4. Have students pair up and quiz each other from their study guides and class notes.

5. Give students an *The Lion, the Witch and the Wardrobe* crossword puzzle to complete.

6. Divide your class into two teams. Use *The Lion, the Witch and the Wardrobe* crossword words with their letters jumbled as a word list. Student 1 from Team A faces off against Student 1 from Team B. You write the first jumbled word on the board. The first student (1A or 1B) to unscramble the word wins the chance for his/her team to score points. If 1A wins the jumble, go to student 2A and give him/her a clue. He/she must give you the correct word which matches that clue. If he/she does, Team A scores a point, and you give student 3A a clue for which you expect another correct response. Continue giving Team A clues until some team member makes an incorrect response. An incorrect response sends the game back to the jumbled-word face off, this time with students 2A and 2B. Instead of repeating giving clues to the first few students of each team, continue with the student after the one who gave the last incorrect response on the team. For example, if Team B wins the jumbled-word face-off, and student 5B gave the last

incorrect answer for Team B, you would start this round of clue questions with student 6B, and so on. The team with the most points wins!

8. Play What's My Line?. This is similar to the old television show. Students assume the roles of different characters from the epic. One student gives clues to the class, or to a panel of contestants. The contestants try to guess the identity of the guest. Students may enjoy assisting you in creating rules and procedures for the game.

9. Play Jeopardy. Divide the class into two groups. Assign each group a category or book from the epic and have them devise answers for that category. Play the game according to the television show procedures.

10. Play Drawing in the Details. This is similar to Pictionary. Divide students into teams. A student from one team draws a scene from the epic. (You may want to specify the Book or section.) Drawings should be kept simple, to keep the pace lively. Students in the opposing team locate the scene in their books and read it aloud. If they are incorrect, the illustrator's team has a chance to guess. Involve students in setting up a scoring system and any other necessary rules.

# UNIT TESTS

# LESSON TWENTY

Objective
To test the students understanding of the main ideas and themes in *The Lion, the Witch and the Wardrobe*

Activity #1
Distribute the unit tests. Go over the instructions in detail and allow the students the entire class period to complete the exam.

NOTES ABOUT THE UNIT TESTS IN THIS UNIT:
There are 5 different unit tests which follow.
There are two short answer tests which are based primarily on facts from the novel. The answer key short answer unit test 1 follows the student test. The answer key for short answer test 2 follows the student short answer unit test 2.
There is one advanced short answer unit test. It is based on the extra discussion questions Use the matching key for short answer unit test 2 to check the matching section of the advanced short answer unit test. There is no key for the short answer questions. The answers will be based on the discussions you have had during class.
There are two multiple choice unit tests. Following the two unit tests, you will find an answer sheet on which students should mark their answers. The same answer sheet should be used for both tests; however, students' answers will be different for each test. Following the students' answer sheet for the multiple choice tests you will find your two keys: one for multiple choice test 1 and one for multiple choice test 2.
The short answer tests have a vocabulary section. You should choose 10 of the vocabulary words from this unit, read them orally and have the students write them down. Then, either have students write a definition or use the words in sentences.

Use these words for the vocabulary section of the advanced short answer unit test:

| inquisitive | jollification | dominions | fraternizing |
| festoons | stratagem | lithe | sluice-gate |
| laburnum | bane | renounced | gibber |

Activity #2
Collect all test papers and assigned books prior to the end of the class period.

# SHORT ANSWER UNIT TEST 1 - *The Lion, the Witch and the Wardrobe*

I. Matching/Identify

   ____  1. Peter          A. the chief of the secret police

   ____  2. Edmund         B. half Jinn, half giantess

   ____  3. Susan          C. the Magnificent

   ____  4. Lucy           D. ashamed to be in the service of the White Witch

   ____  5. White Witch    E. the Valiant

   ____  6. Aslan          F. met all four children in the forest

   ____  7. Mr. Beaver     G. thought logically that Lucy was telling the truth

   ____  8. Mr. Tumnus     H. the Just

   ____  9. Maugrim        I. true King of Narnia

   ____ 10. Professor      J. the Gentle

II. Short Answer

   1. Why were the children sent to the Professor's home?

   2. Describe what Lucy found in the wardrobe.

   3. What did the Witch want Edmund to do?

*The Lion, the Witch and the Wardrobe* Short Answer Unit Test 1 page 2

4. What happened to Mr. Tumnus?

5. What did the prophecy say about the future of Narnia?

6. What did Father Christmas give Peter, Susan, and Lucy?

7. What did the White Witch order Maugrim and his wolves to do?

8. What did Aslan do with Edmund?

9. Describe what happened at the Stone Table.

10. Describe the event of the day after the battle.

*The Lion, the Witch and the Wardrobe* Short Answer Unit Test 1 page 3

III. Essay

    The White Witch owes much of her power to her wand, and once it is broken, her reign crumbles. Explain the significance of the fact that it is Edmund who breaks the wand.

*The Lion, the Witch and the Wardrobe* Short Answer Unit Test 1 page 4

IV. Vocabulary

Write down the vocabulary words. Go back later and write down the correct definition for each word.

1.

2.

3.

4.

5.

6.

7.

8.

9.

10.

SHORT ANSWER UNIT TEST 1 ANSWER KEY - *The Lion, the Witch and the Wardrobe*

I. Matching/Identify

    C   1. Peter            A. the chief of the secret police

    H   2. Edmund           B. half Jinn, half giantess

    J   3. Susan            C. the Magnificent

    E   4. Lucy             D. ashamed to be in the service of the White Witch

    B   5. White Witch      E. the Valiant

    I   6. Aslan            F. met all four children in the forest

    F   7. Mr. Beaver       G. thought logically that Lucy was telling the truth

    D   8. Mr. Tumnus       H. the Just

    A   9. Maugrim          I. true King of Narnia

    G   10. Professor       J. the Gentle

II. Short Answer

1. Why were the children sent to the Professor's home?
    *There were sent away from London during the war because of the air-raids.*

2. Describe what Lucy found in the wardrobe.
    *She found the land of Narnia. She also saw snow, trees, a lamp post.*

3. What did the Witch want Edmund to do?
    *She wanted Edmund to bring his brother and sisters to her house.*

4. What happened to Mr. Tumnus?
    *He was arrested by the White Witch for treason and fraternizing with humans.*

5. What did the prophecy say about the future of Narnia?
    *It said that when two Daughters of Eve and two Sons of Adam sit on the four thrones at Cair Paravel, winter will be over and peace will return to Narnia.*

6. What did Father Christmas give Peter, Susan, and Lucy?
    *Peter was given a sword and a shield. Susan received a bow and arrows and a horn that would bring help when blown. Lucy received a small dagger and a bottle of healing cordial.*

7. What did the White Witch order Maugrim and his wolves to do?
    *She ordered him to take his swiftest wolves, got to the home of the beavers, and kill whatever they would find. If no one was there, they should go to the Stone Table and wait for her in hiding.*

8. What did Aslan do with Edmund?
    *Aslan talked to him in private before bringing him back to his brother and sisters, and all was forgiven.*

9. Describe what happened at the Stone Table.
    *Susan and Lucy looked on from the bushes as the White Witch had Aslan tied and muzzled, shaved, and then bound to the Stone Table where she killed him with a stone knife.*

10. Describe the event of the day after the battle.
    *The children were crowned Kings and Queens of Narnia at Cair Paravel.*


Parts III and IV:

For the essay portion, answers will vary. The vocabulary section will depend upon which words you select from the lists.

# SHORT ANSWER UNIT TEST 2 - *The Lion, the Witch and the Wardrobe*

I. Matching/Identify

____ 1. Lucy          A. the chief of the secret police

____ 2. Mr. Tumnus    B. half Jinn, half giantess

____ 3. Maugrim       C. the Magnificent

____ 4. Aslan         D. ashamed to be in the service of the White Witch

____ 5. White Witch   E. the Valiant

____ 6. Edmund        F. met all four children in the forest

____ 7. Mr. Beaver    G. thought logically that Lucy was telling the truth

____ 8. Peter         H. the Just

____ 9. the Professor I. true King of Narnia

____ 10. Susan        J. the Gentle

II. Short Answer

1. How did the children's adventure begin?

2. Why was Mr. Tumnus crying during Lucy's first visit?

3. Who took the children to safety, and where did they go?

*The Lion, the Witch and the Wardrobe* Short Answer Unit Test 2 page 2

4. Describe the White Witch's reaction to Edmund's arrival at her castle.

5. Why did Aslan show Peter the castle before and of the other children?

6. What did the Deep Magic demand?

7. How was the Witch's spell broken?

8. What did Aslan do to free the statues?

9. Describe the event of the day after the battle.

10. What was the Professor's advice to the children in the end?

*The Lion, the Witch and the Wardrobe* Short Answer Unit Test 2 page 3

III. Composition

Explain the irony of the children's being sent from London to avoid the effects of war only to end up being directly involved in a battle in another world. What might be suggested by Peter's and Edmund's roles in the battle?

*The Lion, the Witch and the Wardrobe* Short Answer Unit Test 2 page 4

IV. Vocabulary

   Write down the vocabulary words. Go back later and write down the correct definitions for the words.

1.

2.

3.

4.

5.

6.

7.

8.

9.

10.

ANSWER KEY: SHORT ANSWER UNIT TEST 2 - *The Lion, the Witch and the Wardrobe*

I. Matching/Identify

E 1. Lucy — A. the chief of the secret police
D 2. Mr. Tumnus — B. half Jinn, half giantess
A 3. Maugrim — C. the Magnificent
I 4. Aslan — D. ashamed to be in the service of the White Witch
B 5. White Witch — E. the Valiant
H 6. Edmund — F. met all four children in the forest
F 7. Mr. Beaver — G. thought logically that Lucy was telling the truth
C 8. Peter — H. the Just
G 9. the Professor — I. true King of Narnia
J 10. Susan — J. the Gentle

II. Short Answer

1. How did the children's adventure begin?
   *Because it was raining, the children could not go outside to explore, so Peter said he was going to explore the house, and the other children agreed.*

2. Why was Mr. Tumnus crying during Lucy's first visit?
   *He did not want to turn Lucy over to the White Witch, but he had taken service under her and was afraid of what she would do if he did not turn a Daughter of Eve over to her, as he had been instructed to do.*

3. Who took the children to safety, and where did they go?
   *Mr. Beaver took them to his dam.*

4. Describe the White Witch's reaction to Edmund's arrival at her castle.
   *She was angry that he had not brought his brother and sisters.*

5. Why did Aslan show Peter the castle before and of the other children?
   *Peter was the firstborn, and he would be High King of all the rest.*

6. What did the Deep Magic demand?
   *The Deep Magic demanded that all traitors belonged to the White Witch as her lawful prey, and that for every treachery she has the right to a kill.*

7. How was the Witch's spell broken?
   *When a willing victim who had committed no treachery was killed in the traitor's stead, the Table would crack and Death itself would start working back ward.*

8. What did Aslan do to free the statues?
   *Aslan breathed on the statues and they returned to life.*

9. Describe the event of the day after the battle.
   *The children were crowned Kings and Queens of Narnia at Cair Paravel.*

10. What was the Professor's advice to the children in the end?
    *He told them not to look to get back into Narnia by the same route.*

Parts III and IV:

For the essay portion, answers will vary. The vocabulary section will depend upon which words you select from the lists.

ADVANCED SHORT ANSWER UNIT TEST - *The Lion, the Witch and the Wardrobe*

I. Matching/Identify

    \_\_\_\_ 1. Lucy                         A. the chief of the secret police

    \_\_\_\_ 2. Mr. Tumnus              B. half Jinn, half giantess

    \_\_\_\_ 3. Maugrim                   C. the Magnificent

    \_\_\_\_ 4. Aslan                       D. ashamed to be in the service of the White Witch

    \_\_\_\_ 5. White Witch             E. the Valiant

    \_\_\_\_ 6. Edmund                  F. met all four children in the forest

    \_\_\_\_ 7. Mr. Beaver               G. thought logically that Lucy was telling the truth

    \_\_\_\_ 8. Peter                       H. the Just

    \_\_\_\_ 9. the Professor            I. true King of Narnia

    \_\_\_\_ 10. Susan                     J. the Gentle

II. Short Answer

1. Where is the climax of the story? Explain your choice.

2. What was Aslan's sacrifice, and why did he do it?

*The Lion, the Witch and the Wardrobe* Advanced Short Answer Unit Test page 2

3. The White Witch owes much of her power to her wand, and once it is broken, her reign crumble. Explain the significance of the fact that it is Edmund who breaks the wand.

4. In ancient myths, the fertility of the land is tied to the health of a heroic figure such as a king or a knight (such as the Fisher King in the Arthurian Legend). The land can be bountiful again only when a spell put on the heroic figure is broken. Explain how *The Lion, the Witch and the Wardrobe* is similar to such a myth. Then explain why the fertility of the land would be of such importance to ancient peoples.

5. Explain the irony of the children being sent from London to avoid the effects of was only to end up being directly involved in a battle in another world. What might be suggested by Peter's and Edmund's roles in the battle?

6. Explain the significance of the fact that each time the children enter Narnia, it is by accident.

*The Lion, the Witch and the Wardrobe* Advanced Short Answer Unit Test page 3

7. Describe the events of the final battle.

8. Explain the steps of the Hero's Journey as it applies to one of the Pevensie children.

*The Lion, the Witch and the Wardrobe* Advanced Short Answer Unit Test page 4

II. Composition
    Discuss the parallels between *The Lion, the Witch and the Wardrobe* and Christianity.

*The Lion, the Witch and the Wardrobe* Advanced Short Answer Unit Test page 5

IV. Vocabulary

    A. Listen to the vocabulary works and write them here. Go back and write a definition for each.

1.

2.

3.

4.

5.

6.

7.

8.

9.

10.

11.

12.

    B. Write a paragraph about *The Lion, the Witch and the Wardrobe* including at least five of the vocabulary words.

MULTIPLE CHOICE UNIT TEST 1 - *The Lion, the Witch and the Wardrobe*

I. Matching

____ 1. Peter            A. the chief of the secret police

____ 2. Edmund           B. half Jinn, half giantess

____ 3. Susan            C. the Magnificent

____ 4. Lucy             D. ashamed to be in the service of the White Witch

____ 5. White Witch      E. the Valiant

____ 6. Aslan            F. met all four children in the forest

____ 7. Mr. Beaver       G. thought logically that Lucy was telling the truth

____ 8. Mr. Tumnus       H. the Just

____ 9. Maugrim          I. true King of Narnia

____ 10. Professor       J. the Gentle

II. Multiple Choice

1. Why were the children sent to the Professor's home?
    A. They were sent there to avoid the air raids in London.
    B. They were orphaned, and the professor was their only living relative.
    C. They'd run away from home and were hiding out there.
    D. They'd been kidnaped by the Professor for ransom.

2. Which of the following is not one of the things Lucy found in the wardrobe?
    A. a lamp post
    B. a place filled with pine trees and snow
    C. a fur coat just her size
    D. a faun

3. What did the Witch want Edmund to do?
    A. She wanted him to come to her castle for the night.
    B. She wanted him to go home and never come back to Narnia.
    C. She wanted him to bring his sisters and brother to her house.
    D. She wanted him to show her the wardrobe.

*Lion, Witch & Wardrobe* Multiple Choice Unit Test 1 page 2

4. What happened to Mr. Tumnus?
    A. He had gone to fetch milk and sardines for the next time Lucy came for tea.
    B. The White Queen had him arrested on charges of treason.
    C. The wolves had killed Mr. Tumnus for fraternizing with humans.
    D. Aslan had arrived and took Mr. Tumnus to safety.

5. Which of the following is not part of the prophecy surrounding Narnia?
    A. That Narnia will forever be frozen in winter
    B. That winter will end when Aslan returns
    C. That peace will reign when the four thrones at Cair Paravel are rightfully filled
    D. That Christmas will not return as long as the White Witch is in power

6. Which of the following are not gifts given to the children by Father Christmas?
    A. A sword and shield
    B. A dagger and a cordial
    C. A bow with arrows and a horn
    D. A crossbow and quiver

7. What did the White Witch order Maugrim and the other wolves to do?
    A. Kill Edmund.
    B. Go to the Beavers' dam and kill everyone they find.
    C. Go to Mr. Tumnus's cave and have him arrested.
    D. Find Aslan and destroy him.

8. What did Aslan do with Edmund?
    A. He talked to him in private and forgave him.
    B. He confronted Edmund angrily about his treachery.
    C. He turned Edmund over to Peter to be tried as a traitor.
    D. He struck Edmund to the ground.

9. What happened at the Stone Table?
    A. The White Witch and her army held a feast before the upcoming battle.
    B. The White Witch humiliated then killed Aslan.
    C. Aslan and the White Witch held a peace conference.
    D. Maugrim recited The Litany Of The Deep Magic.

10. Describe the main event of the day after the battle.
    A. The White Witch was buried.
    B. The children were crowned Kings and Queens of Narnia at Cair Paravel.
    C. The children found their way back to the wardrobe.
    D. The Professor came to Narnia to rescue the children.

*Lion, Witch & Wardrobe* Multiple Choice Unit Test 1 page 3

III. Composition

1. Why does Susan believe that Edmund should never be told of Aslan's sacrifice?

2. The White Witch owes much of her power to her wand, and once it is broken, her reign crumbles. Explain the significance of the fact that it is Edmund who breaks the wand.

3. Explain the irony of the children's being sent from London to avoid the effects of war only to end up being directly involved in a battle in another world. What might be suggested by Peter's and Edmund's roles in the battle?

4. The Professor tells the children that they "won't get into Narnia again by *that* route." What does this and the fact that the Professor believed Lucy to be telling the truth right from the beginning suggest about him?

5. Why do you suppose C. S. Lewis mentions several times that "you should never, never shut yourself in a wardrobe?" What is significant about the one child who does not take this advice?

*Lion, Witch & Wardrobe* Multiple Choice Unit Test 1 page 4

IV. Vocabulary - Match the correct definitions to the words.

_____ 1. pavilion          A. of no exceptional ability

_____ 2. trooped           B. to sharpen a knife

_____ 3. heartily          C. a cloak

_____ 4. melancholy        D. took a risk; dared

_____ 5. ordinary          E. used to lure victims into danger

_____ 6. wretched          F. a place where food is stored

_____ 7. repulsive         G. of little importance or value

_____ 8. mantle            H. offensive; disgusting

_____ 9. sulky             I. to be of use or service to another

_____ 10. disposal         J. to signal or to summon

_____ 11. resumed          K. with warmth or sincerity

_____ 12. whet             L. to put up with; to tolerate

_____ 13. larder           M. not to be relied on; not trustworthy

_____ 14. beckoned         N. sadness or depression of spirits

_____ 15. trifle           O. pouting and withdrawn

_____ 16. solemn           P. to begin again after interruption

_____ 17. treacherous      Q. of poor or mean character

_____ 18. decoy            R. an ornate tent

_____ 19. ventured         S. moved as a group

_____ 20. abide            T. deeply serious and sober

MULTIPLE CHOICE UNIT TEST 2 - *The Lion, the Witch and the Wardrobe*

I. Matching

____ 1. Lucy          A. the chief of the secret police

____ 2. Mr. Tumnus    B. half Jinn, half giantess

____ 3. Maugrim       C. the Magnificent

____ 4. Aslan         D. ashamed to be in the service of the White Witch

____ 5. White Witch   E. the Valiant

____ 6. Edmund        F. met all four children in the forest

____ 7. Mr. Beaver    G. thought logically that Lucy was telling the truth

____ 8. Peter         H. the Just

____ 9. the Professor I. true King of Narnia

____ 10. Susan        J. the Gentle

II. Multiple Choice

1. How did the children's adventure begin?
    A. They found a map in the Professor's office.
    B. They were trying to find a safe place to hide because of the air raids.
    C. It was raining, and they decided to explore the house.
    D. They were setting a trap for the housekeeper.

2. Why was Mr. Tumnus crying during Lucy's first visit?
    A. He was afraid she was hurt after pricking her finger.
    B. He did not want to turn her over to the White Witch now that he knew her.
    C. He was sorry to see her go home after just getting to know her.
    D. The White Witch punished him for trying to trick Lucy.

3. Who took the children to safety, and where did they go?
    A. Mr. Beaver took them to his dam.
    B. Mr. Tumnus took them to his cave.
    C. Father Christmas took them back to the wardrobe.
    D. The White Witch took them to her castle.

*Lion, Witch & Wardrobe* Multiple Choice Unit Test 2 page 2

4. Describe the White Witch's reaction to Edmund's arrival to her castle.
    A. She was happy to see him.
    B. She felt sorry for him because he was hungry, so she gave him Turkish Delight.
    C. She was sad to hear the lies being told about her by the Beaver.
    D. She was angry that he had not brought his brother and sisters.

5. Why did Aslan show Peter the castle before any of the other children?
    A. Aslan wanted to be sure the children would like the castle.
    B. Peter was the firstborn, and he would be High King of all the rest.
    C. Lucy and Susan were tired and went to sleep.
    D. Aslan wanted to impress Peter.

6. What did the Deep Magic demand?
    A. All traitors must be turned over to the White Witch as her lawful prey.
    B. Each time the White Witch met Aslan, he had to bow to her.
    C. Aslan could do anything he chose because he was king.
    D. No meeting should take place before sundown.

7. How was the Witch's spell broken?
    A. Lucy and Susan said magic words that brought Aslan back to life.
    B. Aslan willingly gave his life for Edmund, the traitor, so the spell was broken.
    C. Edmund gave the White Witch gold to bring Aslan back to life.
    D. When Peter became a Knight he had the power to bring Aslan back to life.

8. What did Aslan do to free the statues?
    A. Aslan killed the White Witch, which automatically freed the statues.
    B. Aslan poured a cordial on them.
    C. Aslan breathed on the statues, and they returned to life.
    D. Aslan had Susan blow her horn.

9. Describe the event of the day after the battle.
    A. The White Witch was buried
    B. The children were crowned Kings and Queens of Narnia at Cair Paravel.
    C. The children found their way back to the wardrobe.
    D. The Professor came to Narnia to rescue the children.

10. What was the Professor's advice to the children in the end?
    A. He told them to go back to the wardrobe anytime to go to Narnia.
    B. He told them not to believe everything they see.
    C. He told them not to look to get back to Narnia by the same route.
    D. He told them to get some sleep because they were tired from their busy day.

*Lion, Witch & Wardrobe* Multiple Choice Unit Test 2 page 3

III. Composition

1. Discuss the significance of each of the names the Pevensie children receive at their coronoation. How does each fit the character and why?

2. Discuss the gifts that the children received from Father Christmas. How was each used in *The Lion, the Witch and the Wardrobe*?

3. Although C. S. Lewis denied that Aslan's sacrifice in *The Lion, the Witch and the Wardrobe* is a direct allegory to the Passion of Jesus Christ, many parallels can be drawn. Compare and contrast the two events.

4. Compare and contrast the Pevensie children's return from Narnia to Dorothy's return from Oz in *The Wonderful Wizard of Oz* by L. Frank Baum. Just because both adventures could be remembered as if only dreams, does that make the journey any less significant? Explain why or why not.

5. Suppose one of the other Pevensie children had gone into the wardrobe first. How might the story have been different if Edmund had been the first to meet Mr. Tumnus? What if Peter had been the one to meet the White Witch instead of Edmund? What if Susan was first?

*Lion, Witch & Wardrobe* Multiple Choice Unit Test 2 page 4

IV. Vocabulary - Match the correct definitions to the words.

| | | | |
|---|---|---|---|
| _____ | 1. foreboding | A. | showing ill will and a desire to hurt |
| _____ | 2. incantation | B. | a military operation or plan |
| _____ | 3. din | C. | a building and its grounds |
| _____ | 4. alliance | D. | a state of joyful exuberance or merriment |
| _____ | 5. stag | E. | a sense of impending evil or misfortune |
| _____ | 6. centaur | F. | very disagreeable; unpleasant |
| _____ | 7. campaign | G. | the adult male of various deer |
| _____ | 8. velvet | H. | political partnership |
| _____ | 9. muffler | I. | a tree branch, especially a large or main branch |
| _____ | 10. gaiety | J. | believed to have a magical effect; a spell |
| _____ | 11. parcel | K. | something wrapped up or packaged |
| _____ | 12. sledge | L. | structures that taper to a point at the top |
| _____ | 13. spires | M. | to cause to sleep or rest; soothe or calm |
| _____ | 14. token | N. | to cover over with a soft, furry covering |
| _____ | 15. bough | O. | something serving as proof of something else; a sign |
| _____ | 16. premises | P. | vehicle drawn by work animals across ice or snow |
| _____ | 17. beastly | Q. | a loud harsh noise |
| _____ | 18. hoax | R. | an act intended to deceive or trick |
| _____ | 19. lulling | S. | a heavy scarf worn around the neck for warmth |
| _____ | 20. spiteful | T. | a mythical being that is half man and half horse |

ANSWER SHEET - *The Lion, the Witch and the Wardrobe*
Multiple Choice Unit Tests

| I. Matching | II. Multiple Choice | IV. Vocabulary |
|---|---|---|
| 1. ___ | 1. ___ | 1. ___ |
| 2. ___ | 2. ___ | 2. ___ |
| 3. ___ | 3. ___ | 3. ___ |
| 4. ___ | 4. ___ | 4. ___ |
| 5. ___ | 5. ___ | 5. ___ |
| 6. ___ | 6. ___ | 6. ___ |
| 7. ___ | 7. ___ | 7. ___ |
| 8. ___ | 8. ___ | 8. ___ |
| 9. ___ | 9. ___ | 9. ___ |
| 10. ___ | 10. ___ | 10. ___ |
| | 11. ___ | 11. ___ |
| | 12. ___ | 12. ___ |
| | 13. ___ | 13. ___ |
| | 14. ___ | 14. ___ |
| | 15. ___ | 15. ___ |
| | 16. ___ | 16. ___ |
| | 17. ___ | 17. ___ |
| | 18. ___ | 18. ___ |
| | 19. ___ | 19. ___ |
| | 20. ___ | 20. ___ |
| | 21. ___ | |
| | 22. ___ | |
| | 23. ___ | |
| | 24. ___ | |
| | 25. ___ | |

## ANSWER KEY - *The Lion, the Witch and the Wardrobe*
## Multiple Choice Unit Test 1

| I. Matching | II. Multiple Choice | IV. Vocabulary |
|---|---|---|
| 1. C | 1. A | 1. R |
| 2. H | 2. C | 2. S |
| 3. J | 3. C | 3. K |
| 4. E | 4. B | 4. N |
| 5. B | 5. A | 5. A |
| 6. I | 6. D | 6. Q |
| 7. F | 7. B | 7. H |
| 8. D | 8. A | 8. C |
| 9. A | 9. B | 9. O |
| 10. G | 10. B | 10. I |
| | | 11. P |
| | | 12. B |
| | | 13. F |
| | | 14. J |
| | | 15. G |
| | | 16. T |
| | | 17. M |
| | | 18. E |
| | | 19. D |
| | | 20. L |

# ANSWER KEY - *The Lion, the Witch and the Wardrobe*
## Multiple Choice Unit Test 2

| I. Matching | II. Multiple Choice | IV. Vocabulary |
|---|---|---|
| 1. E | 1. C | 1. E |
| 2. D | 2. B | 2. J |
| 3. A | 3. A | 3. Q |
| 4. I | 4. D | 4. H |
| 5. B | 5. B | 5. G |
| 6. H | 6. A | 6. T |
| 7. F | 7. B | 7. B |
| 8. C | 8. C | 8. N |
| 9. G | 9. B | 9. S |
| 10. J | 10. C | 10. D |
| | | 11. K |
| | | 12. P |
| | | 13. L |
| | | 14. O |
| | | 15. I |
| | | 16. C |
| | | 17. F |
| | | 18. R |
| | | 19. M |
| | | 20. A |

# UNIT RESOURCE MATERIALS

# BULLETIN BOARD IDEAS - *The Lion, the Witch and the Wardrobe*

1. Save one corner of the board for the best of students' *The Lion, the Witch and the Wardrobe* writing assignments.

2. Take one of the word search puzzles from the extra activities packet and with a marker copy it over in a large size on the bulletin board. Write the clue words to find to one side. Invite students prior to and after class to find the words and circle them on the bulletin board.

3. Write several of the most significant quotations from the book onto the board on brightly colored paper.

4. Make a bulletin board listing the vocabulary words for this unit. As you complete sections of the novel and discuss the vocabulary for each section, write the definitions on the bulletin board. (If your board is one students face frequently, it will help them learn the words.)

5. Create a bulletin board based on Joseph Campbell's "The Hero's Journey" pattern and relate it to the Pevensie children.

6. Create a memorial bulletin board about the Blitz on London during World War II and the terrorist attacks on 9/11/2001.

7. Have students decorate a bulletin board with family crests that they have designed.

8. Display the poems written during Lesson Five complete with pictures that support the idea of resisting temptation.

9. Display the students' WebQuest projects.

## EXTRA ACTIVITIES - *The Lion, the Witch and the Wardrobe*

One of the difficulties in teaching a novel is that all students don't read at the same speed. One student who likes to read may take the book home and finish it in a day or two. Sometimes a few students finish the in-class assignments early. The problem, then, is finding suitable extra activities for students.

One thing that seems to help is to keep a little library in the classroom. For this unit on *The Lion, the Witch and the Wardrobe*, you might check out from the school library C. S. Lewis' other Narnia books: *The Magician's Nephew, The Horse and His Boy, Prince Caspian, the Voyage of the Dawn Treader, The Silver Chair,* or *The Last Battle.* Books with similar themes about fantasy might include: J. R. R. Tolkien's *Lord of the Rings* Trilogy (*The Fellowship of the Ring, The Two Towers,* and *The Return of the King)* or *The Hobbit* or J. K. Rowling's *Harry Potter* series (*The Sorcerer's Stone, The Chamber of Secrets, The Prisoner of Azkaban, The Goblet of Fire, The Order of the Pheonix,* or *The Half-Blood Prince*). Any stories or articles about World War II, the stories from New Testament, or contemporary heroes could also be of interest.

Other things you may keep on hand are puzzles. We have made some relating directly to *The Lion, the Witch and the Wardrobe* for you. Feel free to duplicate them for your students to use.

Some students may like to draw. You might devise a contest or allow some extra-credit grade for students who draw characters or scenes from *The Lion, the Witch and the Wardrobe*. Note, too, that if the students do not want to keep their drawings you may pick up some extra bulletin board materials this way. If you have a contest and you supply the prize (a CD or something like that perhaps), you could, possibly, make the drawing itself a non-returnable entry fee.

The pages which follow contain games, puzzles and worksheets. The keys, when appropriate, immediately follow the puzzle or worksheet. There are two main groups of activities: one group for the unit; that is, generally relating to *The Lion, the Witch and the Wardrobe* text, and another group of activities related strictly to *The Lion, the Witch and the Wardrobe* vocabulary.

Directions for these games, puzzles and worksheets are self-explanatory. The object here is to provide you with extra materials you may use in any way you choose.

# MORE ACTIVITIES - *The Lion, the Witch and the Wardrobe*

1. Have students work together to make a time line chronology of the events in the story. Take a large piece of construction paper and on one wall (or however you can physically arrange it in your room) and make the events of the story along it. Students may want to add drawings or cut-out pictures to represent the events (as well as a written statement).

2. Have students design a book cover (front and back and inside flaps) for *The Lion, the Witch and the Wardrobe*.

3. Have students design a bulletin board (ready to be put up; not just sketched) for *The Lion, the Witch and the Wardrobe*.

4. Have students choose one chapter of the book (with sufficient dialogue) to rewrite as a play. In conjunction with this assignment, have students write a composition explaining the difficulties they encountered in changing from one written form to another.

6. Have students create a bulletin board size map of Narnia and outline the journey of the Pevensie children.

7. Have students research the sources for the mythological creatures in the novel.

8. The Professor used logic to determine that Lucy was not mad nor lying. Using the Internet, find logic puzzles for the class.

9. Have students predict the story the Professor's relationship to the Narnia tale and then read *The Magician's Nephew*.

# WORD SEARCH - The Lion, The Witch & The Wardrobe

Words are placed backwards, forward, diagonally, up and down. Words listed below are included in the maze. Circle the hidden vocabulary words in the maze.

```
P R O F E S S O R G T V C S R S N V P Z
R U M B L E B U F F I N C S D S M Y W Q
L G F S Z K Q P H T T S W C V K V Y T V
A W Z S K R B P K P A B Z M G Y D F B L
I G P U R K Z K V R N F E T T K A J K C
D M H N D N T S D H A R B A F S G C L G
R L Q M R I P I R H L A L W V W G K N W
O M N U D F N V R S S W X E O E E D O Y
C A S T L E M C R E A D Y C U L R B D M
X Z X O S Q O A I U D J C I Q O V S T V
B Z W R G A S V A T T M C M W B Q E D J
V V S H T J P E C A Z L U S K A Q M S L
H N L S G X R Z S T P R T N F T W A N V
O V E H M P I T H S E A Q O D T A U M V
R S D W F M N D I T G S T W T L R G R H
N S G S A G G C E N T A U R S E D R H V
M G E K U N F P L M L M R F V T R I C C
W F L X R S D L D X O T K K C B O M K N
G P A P C T A C V H N S I W Y N B N S D
G S M U G Z Q N C S D I S F F N E L E Z
Z D P Q N C C T C B O R H N X J F P J D
Y P K V Y D I Y Y N N H Q D K S J Z S P
P L S R Q W N L T Y R C F M P N M L D Z
```

| | | | | |
|---|---|---|---|---|
| ASLAN | COATS | LONDON | SHIELD | TUMNUS |
| BATTLE | CORDIAL | LUCY | SLEDGE | TURKISH |
| BEAVERS | DAGGER | MAUGRIM | SNOW | WAND |
| BOW | DWARF | MCREADY | SPRING | WARDROBE |
| CAIR | EDMUND | MICE | STAG | WITCH |
| CASTLE | FAUN | PETER | STATUES | WOLF |
| CAVE | HORN | PROFESSOR | STONE | WOLVES |
| CENTAUR | KNIFE | RUMBLEBUFFIN | SUSAN | |
| CHRISTMAS | LAMP | SARDINES | SWORD | |

WORD SEARCH ANSWER KEY - The Lion, The Witch & The Wardrobe

Words are placed backwards, forward, diagonally, up and down. Words listed below are included in the maze. Circle the hidden vocabulary words in the maze.

| | | | | | | | | | | | | | | | | | | | |
|---|---|---|---|---|---|---|---|---|---|---|---|---|---|---|---|---|---|---|---|
| P | R | O | F | E | S | S | O | R | | | | | | | | | | | |
| R | U | M | B | L | E | B | U | F | F | I | N | | | | | | | | |
| L | | | | | | | | | | | S | | | | | | | | |
| A | | | S | | | | | | | A | B | | | | | D | | | |
| I | | | U | | K | | | | R | N | F | E | | | | A | | | |
| D | | | N | | N | | | D | | A | R | | A | | | G | | | |
| R | | | M | | I | | I | | | L | A | | W | V | | G | | | W |
| O | | | U | | F | N | | | S | S | W | | E | O | E | E | D | O | |
| C | A | S | T | L | E | M | C | R | E | A | D | Y | C | U | L | R | B | | |
| | | | O | S | | O | A | I | U | D | | | I | | O | V | S | | |
| | | W | | | A | S | V | A | T | | M | | M | W | B | | E | | |
| | | S | | T | | P | E | C | A | | | U | S | | A | | M | S | |
| H | | L | S | | | R | | S | T | | R | T | N | | T | W | A | | |
| O | | E | | | | I | | H | S | E | A | | O | D | T | A | U | | |
| R | | D | W | | | N | | I | T | G | S | T | W | | L | R | G | | |
| N | | G | S | A | | G | C | E | N | T | A | U | R | S | E | D | R | | |
| | | E | | U | N | | P | L | | L | M | R | | | T | R | I | | |
| | F | L | | | S | D | | D | | O | T | K | | | | O | M | | |
| | | A | | | | A | | | H | N | S | I | | | | B | N | | |
| | | M | U | | | | N | C | | D | I | S | | | | E | | E | |
| | | P | | N | | | T | | | O | R | H | | | | | | | |
| | | | | | | I | | | | N | H | | | | | | | | |
| | | | | | W | | | | | | C | | | | | | | | |

| | | | | |
|---|---|---|---|---|
| ASLAN | COATS | LONDON | SHIELD | TUMNUS |
| BATTLE | CORDIAL | LUCY | SLEDGE | TURKISH |
| BEAVERS | DAGGER | MAUGRIM | SNOW | WAND |
| BOW | DWARF | MCREADY | SPRING | WARDROBE |
| CAIR | EDMUND | MICE | STAG | WITCH |
| CASTLE | FAUN | PETER | STATUES | WOLF |
| CAVE | HORN | PROFESSOR | STONE | WOLVES |
| CENTAUR | KNIFE | RUMBLEBUFFIN | SUSAN | |
| CHRISTMAS | LAMP | SARDINES | SWORD | |

# CROSSWORD - The Lion, The Witch & The Wardrobe

Across
1. Susan's unused gift: ___ and arrow
3. They gnawed through Aslan's ropes.
4. First to enter Narnia
8. He gave useful gifts to the children: Father ___
12. Short servant of the White Witch
13. Place of sacrifice; ___ Table
14. Used to kill Maugrim
15. She was half Jinn & half giantess; White ___
17. Lucy met Mr. Tumnus at the ___ post.
18. He destroyed winter & killed the Witch.
20. Nature's white winter covering
21. Children borrowed these from the wardrobe
22. White Witch's transportation

Down
1. They took the children to Aslan.
2. Edmund broke the White Witch's
3. Chief of the secret police
5. Used to save the wounded after the battle
6. Doorway to Narnia
7. Witch used it to kill Aslan
8. Mr. Tumnus's house was a ___.
9. Edmund's temptation: ___ Delight
10. It was located between two mountains: Witch's ___
11. Home town of the Pevensie children
14. It arrived with Aslan.
15. Attacked Susan and Lucy
16. The Faun who had tea with Lucy
19. Hunted by the adult Pevensies; White ___

# CROSSWORD ANSWER KEY - The Lion, The Witch & The Wardrobe

|   |   | 1 B | O | 2 W |   |   |   |   |   |   |   |   |
|---|---|---|---|---|---|---|---|---|---|---|---|---|
| 3 M | I | C | E | A |   | 4 L | 5 C | Y |   |   |   |   |
| A |   | A |   | N |   | O |   |   |   | 6 W |   | 7 K |
| U |   | V |   | D |   | 8 C | H | R | I | S | T | M | A | S |   | N |
| G |   | E |   |   |   | A |   | D |   | 9 T |   | R | 10 C |   | I |
| R |   | R |   | 11 L | V | I |   |   |   | R |   | 12 D | W | A | R | F |
| I |   | 13 S | T | O | N | E |   | A |   | K |   | R | S |   | E |
| M |   |   |   | N |   |   |   | L |   | I |   | O | T |   |   |
|   | 14 S | W | O | R | D |   |   |   |   | S |   | B | L |   |   |
|   | P |   |   | O |   | 15 W | I | 16 T | C | H |   | E | E |   |   |
|   | R |   |   | N |   | O |   | U |   |   |   |   |   |   |   |
|   | I |   |   |   |   | 17 L | A | M | P |   | 18 A | 19 S | L | A | N |
| 20 S | N | O | W |   |   | V |   | N |   |   | T |   |   |   |   |
|   | G |   |   |   |   | E |   | U |   |   | A |   |   |   |   |
|   |   |   | 21 C | O | A | T | S |   | 22 S | L | E | D | G | E |

## Across

1. Susan's unused gift: ___ and arrow
3. They gnawed through Aslan's ropes.
4. First to enter Narnia
8. He gave useful gifts to the children: Father ___
12. Short servant of the White Witch
13. Place of sacrifice; ___ Table
14. Used to kill Maugrim
15. She was half Jinn & half giantess; White ___
17. Lucy met Mr. Tumnus at the ___ post.
18. He destroyed winter & killed the Witch.
20. Nature's white winter covering
21. Children borrowed these from the wardrobe
22. White Witch's transportation

## Down

1. They took the children to Aslan.
2. Edmund broke the White Witch's
3. Chief of the secret police
5. Used to save the wounded after the battle
6. Doorway to Narnia
7. Witch used it to kill Aslan
8. Mr. Tumnus's house was a ___.
9. Edmund's temptation: ___ Delight
10. It was located between two mountains: Witch's ___
11. Home town of the Pevensie children
14. It arrived with Aslan.
15. Attacked Susan and Lucy
16. The Faun who had tea with Lucy
19. Hunted by the adult Pevensies; White ___

MATCHING 1 - The Lion, The Witch & The Wardrobe

___ 1. CASTLE             A. She was half Jinn & half giantess; White ___
___ 2. CORDIAL            B. Doorway to Narnia
___ 3. SHIELD             C. It contained a red lion crest.
___ 4. SLEDGE             D. Mr. Tumnus's house was a ___.
___ 5. WOLF               E. White Witch's transportation
___ 6. CAVE               F. Sir Peter ____'s Bane
___ 7. WITCH              G. Lucy met Mr. Tumnus at the ___ post.
___ 8. PROFESSOR          H. Owner of the country house where the children stayed
___ 9. MAUGRIM            I. It arrived with Aslan.
___10. LAMP               J. Nature's white winter covering
___11. LUCY               K. First to enter Narnia
___12. LONDON             L. Used to save the wounded after the battle
___13. SNOW               M. Aslan's breath freed these.
___14. PETER              N. Witch used it to kill Aslan
___15. EDMUND             O. Lucy's gift that she did not use
___16. SARDINES           P. He killed Maugrim.
___17. STAG               Q. ___ The Just
___18. WARDROBE           R. Tea-time treat
___19. RUMBLEBUFFIN       S. A friendly giant
___20. STATUES            T. They took the children to Aslan.
___21. TUMNUS             U. Home town of the Pevensie children
___22. SPRING             V. Hunted by the adult Pevensies; White ___
___23. KNIFE              W. It was located between two mountains: Witch's ___
___24. BEAVERS            X. Chief of the secret police
___25. DAGGER             Y. The Faun who had tea with Lucy

MATCHING 1 ANSWER KEY - The Lion, The Witch & The Wardrobe

W  1. CASTLE          A. She was half Jinn & half giantess; White ___
L - 2. CORDIAL        B. Doorway to Narnia
C - 3. SHIELD         C. It contained a red lion crest.
E - 4. SLEDGE         D. Mr. Tumnus's house was a ___.
F - 5. WOLF           E. White Witch's transportation
D - 6. CAVE           F. Sir Peter ____'s Bane
A - 7. WITCH          G. Lucy met Mr. Tumnus at the ___ post.
H - 8. PROFESSOR      H. Owner of the country house where the children stayed
X - 9. MAUGRIM        I. It arrived with Aslan.
G -10. LAMP           J. Nature's white winter covering
K -11. LUCY           K. First to enter Narnia
U -12. LONDON         L. Used to save the wounded after the battle
J -13. SNOW           M. Aslan's breath freed these.
P -14. PETER          N. Witch used it to kill Aslan
Q -15. EDMUND         O. Lucy's gift that she did not use
R -16. SARDINES       P. He killed Maugrim.
V -17. STAG           Q. ___ The Just
B -18. WARDROBE       R. Tea-time treat
S -19. RUMBLEBUFFIN   S. A friendly giant
M -20. STATUES        T. They took the children to Aslan.
Y -21. TUMNUS         U. Home town of the Pevensie children
I -22. SPRING         V. Hunted by the adult Pevensies; White ___
N -23. KNIFE          W. It was located between two mountains: Witch's ___
T -24. BEAVERS        X. Chief of the secret police
O -25. DAGGER         Y. The Faun who had tea with Lucy

# MATCHING 2 - The Lion, The Witch & The Wardrobe

___ 1. PROFESSOR         A. He gave useful gifts to the children: Father ___
___ 2. LUCY              B. The Faun who had tea with Lucy
___ 3. STONE             C. Susan's unused gift: ___ and arrow
___ 4. STATUES           D. Witch used it to kill Aslan
___ 5. CHRISTMAS         E. Mr. Tumnus's race
___ 6. FAUN              F. Hunted by the adult Pevensies; White ___
___ 7. STAG              G. Attacked Susan and Lucy
___ 8. TUMNUS            H. Used to kill Maugrim
___ 9. SPRING            I. Castle by the sea; ___ Paravel
___ 10. BEAVERS          J. It arrived with Aslan.
___ 11. LAMP             K. Tea-time treat
___ 12. SARDINES         L. Doorway to Narnia
___ 13. BOW              M. He destroyed winter & killed the Witch.
___ 14. KNIFE            N. She told the children to stay out of trouble.
___ 15. CORDIAL          O. Aslan's breath freed these.
___ 16. MICE             P. Susan used this to call for help.
___ 17. WARDROBE         Q. They took the children to Aslan.
___ 18. BATTLE           R. They gnawed through Aslan's ropes.
___ 19. WOLVES           S. Lucy met Mr. Tumnus at the ___ post.
___ 20. ASLAN            T. Aslan and Peter planned this after the White Witch left camp.
___ 21. HORN             U. A friendly giant
___ 22. MCREADY          V. Owner of the country house where the children stayed
___ 23. CAIR             W. Used to save the wounded after the battle
___ 24. RUMBLEBUFFIN     X. First to enter Narnia
___ 25. SWORD            Y. Place of sacrifice; ___ Table

## MATCHING 2 ANSWER KEY - The Lion, The Witch & The Wardrobe

| | | |
|---|---|---|
| V - 1. PROFESSOR | A. | He gave useful gifts to the children: Father ___ |
| X - 2. LUCY | B. | The Faun who had tea with Lucy |
| Y - 3. STONE | C. | Susan's unused gift: ___ and arrow |
| O - 4. STATUES | D. | Witch used it to kill Aslan |
| A - 5. CHRISTMAS | E. | Mr. Tumnus's race |
| E - 6. FAUN | F. | Hunted by the adult Pevensies; White ___ |
| F - 7. STAG | G. | Attacked Susan and Lucy |
| B - 8. TUMNUS | H. | Used to kill Maugrim |
| J - 9. SPRING | I. | Castle by the sea; ___ Paravel |
| Q -10. BEAVERS | J. | It arrived with Aslan. |
| S -11. LAMP | K. | Tea-time treat |
| K -12. SARDINES | L. | Doorway to Narnia |
| C -13. BOW | M. | He destroyed winter & killed the Witch. |
| D -14. KNIFE | N. | She told the children to stay out of trouble. |
| W  15. CORDIAL | O. | Aslan's breath freed these. |
| R -16. MICE | P. | Susan used this to call for help. |
| L -17. WARDROBE | Q. | They took the children to Aslan. |
| T -18. BATTLE | R. | They gnawed through Aslan's ropes. |
| G -19. WOLVES | S. | Lucy met Mr. Tumnus at the ___ post. |
| M  20. ASLAN | T. | Aslan and Peter planned this after the White Witch left camp. |
| P -21. HORN | U. | A friendly giant |
| N -22. MCREADY | V. | Owner of the country house where the children stayed |
| I - 23. CAIR | W. | Used to save the wounded after the battle |
| U -24. RUMBLEBUFFIN | X. | First to enter Narnia |
| H -25. SWORD | Y. | Place of sacrifice; ___ Table |

## JUGGLE LETTERS - The Lion, The Witch, & The Wardrobe

1. AECV = 1. _____
   Mr. Tumnus's house was a ___.

2. OSWLVE = 2. _____
   Attacked Susan and Lucy

3. RDCAMYE = 3. _____
   She told the children to stay out of trouble.

4. NMSTUU = 4. _____
   The Faun who had tea with Lucy

5. PSNRGI = 5. _____
   It arrived with Aslan.

6. RESABVE = 6. _____
   They took the children to Aslan.

7. NDESISRA = 7. _____
   Tea-time treat

8. CULY = 8. _____
   First to enter Narnia

9. PMLA = 9. _____
   Lucy met Mr. Tumnus at the ___ post.

10. ASTLEC =10. _____
    It was located between two mountains: Witch's ___

11. RCAI =11. _____
    Castle by the sea; ___ Paravel

12. TSCOA =12. _____
    Children borrowed these from the wardrobe

13. ETPER =13. _____
    He killed Maugrim.

14. SANAL =14. _____
    He destroyed winter & killed the Witch.

15. AEDRBROW =15. _____
    Doorway to Narnia

16. RDILCAO =16. _____
Used to save the wounded after the battle

17. NMDUDE =17. _____
___ The Just

18. WOB =18. _____
Susan's unused gift: ___ and arrow

19. USNAS =19. _____
She carried a horn.

20. UAMRGMI =20. _____
Chief of the secret police

21. EDLGSE =21. _____
White Witch's transportation

22. HIDESL =22. _____
It contained a red lion crest.

23. NROH =23. _____
Susan used this to call for help.

24. TSEAUST =24. _____
Aslan's breath freed these.

25. NONODL =25. _____
Home town of the Pevensie children

26. NWOS =26. _____
Nature's white winter covering

27. LFWO =27. _____
Sir Peter ____'s Bane

28. ASHMRITCS =28. _____
He gave useful gifts to the children: Father ___

29. EGRADG =29. _____
Lucy's gift that she did not use

30. TSGA =30. _____
Hunted by the adult Pevensies; White ___

31. LTBATE =31. _____
Aslan and Peter planned this after the White Witch left camp.

32. ICEM =32. _____
They gnawed through Aslan's ropes.

33. SHRUTKI =33. _____
Edmund's temptation: ___ Delight

34. BFUIMBELNRFU =34. _____
A friendly giant

35. AWDN =35. _____
Edmund broke the White Witch's

36. DRWOS =36. _____
Used to kill Maugrim

37. UNAF =37. _____
Mr. Tumnus's race

38. RDWAF =38. _____
Short servant of the White Witch

39. TWIHC =39. _____
She was half Jinn & half giantess; White ___

40. FSRRPEOOS =40. _____
Owner of the country house where the children stayed

## JUGGLE LETTERS ANSWER KEY - The Lion, The Witch, & The Wardrobe

1. AECV = 1. CAVE
   Mr. Tumnus's house was a ___.

2. OSWLVE = 2. WOLVES
   Attacked Susan and Lucy

3. RDCAMYE = 3. MCREADY
   She told the children to stay out of trouble.

4. NMSTUU = 4. TUMNUS
   The Faun who had tea with Lucy

5. PSNRGI = 5. SPRING
   It arrived with Aslan.

6. RESABVE = 6. BEAVERS
   They took the children to Aslan.

7. NDESISRA = 7. SARDINES
   Tea-time treat

8. CULY = 8. LUCY
   First to enter Narnia

9. PMLA = 9. LAMP
   Lucy met Mr. Tumnus at the ___ post.

10. ASTLEC =10. CASTLE
    It was located between two mountains: Witch's ___

11. RCAI =11. CAIR
    Castle by the sea; ___ Paravel

12. TSCOA =12. COATS
    Children borrowed these from the wardrobe

13. ETPER =13. PETER
    He killed Maugrim.

14. SANAL =14. ASLAN
    He destroyed winter & killed the Witch.

15. AEDRBROW =15. WARDROBE
    Doorway to Narnia

16. RDILCAO =16. CORDIAL
Used to save the wounded after the battle

17. NMDUDE =17. EDMUND
\_\_\_ The Just

18. WOB =18. BOW
Susan's unused gift: \_\_\_ and arrow

19. USNAS =19. SUSAN
She carried a horn.

20. UAMRGMI =20. MAUGRIM
Chief of the secret police

21. EDLGSE =21. SLEDGE
White Witch's transportation

22. HIDESL =22. SHIELD
It contained a red lion crest.

23. NROH =23. HORN
Susan used this to call for help.

24. TSEAUST =24. STATUES
Aslan's breath freed these.

25. NONODL =25. LONDON
Home town of the Pevensie children

26. NWOS =26. SNOW
Nature's white winter covering

27. LFWO =27. WOLF
Sir Peter \_\_\_\_'s Bane

28. ASHMRITCS =28. CHRISTMAS
He gave useful gifts to the children: Father \_\_\_

29. EGRADG =29. DAGGER
Lucy's gift that she did not use

30. TSGA =30. STAG
Hunted by the adult Pevensies; White \_\_\_

31. LTBATE =31. BATTLE
Aslan and Peter planned this after the White Witch left camp.

32. ICEM =32. MICE
They gnawed through Aslan's ropes.

33. SHRUTKI =33. TURKISH
Edmund's temptation: ___ Delight

34. BFUIMBELNRFU =34. RUMBLEBUFFIN
A friendly giant

35. AWDN =35. WAND
Edmund broke the White Witch's

36. DRWOS =36. SWORD
Used to kill Maugrim

37. UNAF =37. FAUN
Mr. Tumnus's race

38. RDWAF =38. DWARF
Short servant of the White Witch

39. TWIHC =39. WITCH
She was half Jinn & half giantess; White ___

40. FSRRPEOOS =40. PROFESSOR
Owner of the country house where the children stayed

# VOCABULARY RESOURCE MATERIALS

# VOCABULARY WORD SEARCH - The Lion, The Witch, & The Wardrobe

```
M U N R U B A L L I A N C E Z C Y Y D I
S E S I M E R P G G B G S T B O F L K N
G Q N P T A C N J S N F L N C Z Q P M C
X U X D I S I Z J I G W E E Y L Y A B A
G A T S A T Y R R B I C D O M I N I O N
P R K V H L E E E E A L G X F T O R O T
E R K G P Y E F S C P N E K L H T I P A
D Y I I R J S R U W M U E E R E T S R T
L L F N O N O E M L A F L E J A U P O I
A N A Q P Y L C E U C R G S C F L I D O
R S B U H D E K D S F G D I I N G R I N
S J I I E C M O V L I F F R T V Y E G W
N W D S C J N N J N A I L U O W E S I B
O H E I Y D P E S J L R R E J B Q T O X
O E W T L E A D R L N R D S R Y E J U P
T T S I U T R O O P E D V E L V E T S T
S X H V L T C J H T K C I L R U M Q F Z
E N O E L A E Y P Y O F I S R S I S T N
F B R Z I R L G M B T R R T P A U C N R
D I N C N D S P A G H O A X S O B L E G
E D A L G G C Z C S P R I N G Y S B K P
G I B B E R H E A R T I L Y W R P A L Y
E N C H A N T E D E C N U O N E R N L E
```

| ABIDE | ENCHANTED | LARDER | RECKONED | SPITEFUL |
| ALIGHTING | FESTOONS | LITHE | RENOUNCED | SPRINGY |
| ALLIANCE | GIBBER | LULLING | REPULSIVE | STAG |
| BANE | GLADE | MANTLE | RESUMED | SULKY |
| BEASTLY | GLUTTONY | MUFFLER | SATYR | TOKEN |
| CAMPAIGN | HEARTILY | PARCELS | SHORN | TROOPED |
| CAMPHOR | HOAX | PEDLARS | SHRILL | TURRET |
| DECOY | INCANTATION | PREMISES | SLEDGE | VELVET |
| DIN | INQUISITIVE | PRODIGIOUS | SLUICE | WARDROBE |
| DISPOSAL | JEERING | PROPHECY | SNIGGER | WHET |
| DOMINION | JOLLIFICATION | QUARRY | SOLEMN | |
| DRATTED | LABURNUM | RABBLE | SPIRES | |

# VOCABULARY WORD SEARCH ANSWER KEY - The Lion, The Witch, & The Wardrobe

| ABIDE | ENCHANTED | LARDER | RECKONED | SPITEFUL |
| ALIGHTING | FESTOONS | LITHE | RENOUNCED | SPRINGY |
| ALLIANCE | GIBBER | LULLING | REPULSIVE | STAG |
| BANE | GLADE | MANTLE | RESUMED | SULKY |
| BEASTLY | GLUTTONY | MUFFLER | SATYR | TOKEN |
| CAMPAIGN | HEARTILY | PARCELS | SHORN | TROOPED |
| CAMPHOR | HOAX | PEDLARS | SHRILL | TURRET |
| DECOY | INCANTATION | PREMISES | SLEDGE | VELVET |
| DIN | INQUISITIVE | PRODIGIOUS | SLUICE | WARDROBE |
| DISPOSAL | JEERING | PROPHECY | SNIGGER | WHET |
| DOMINION | JOLLIFICATION | QUARRY | SOLEMN | |
| DRATTED | LABURNUM | RABBLE | SPIRES | |

# VOCABULARY CROSSWORD - The Lion, The Witch, & The Wardrobe

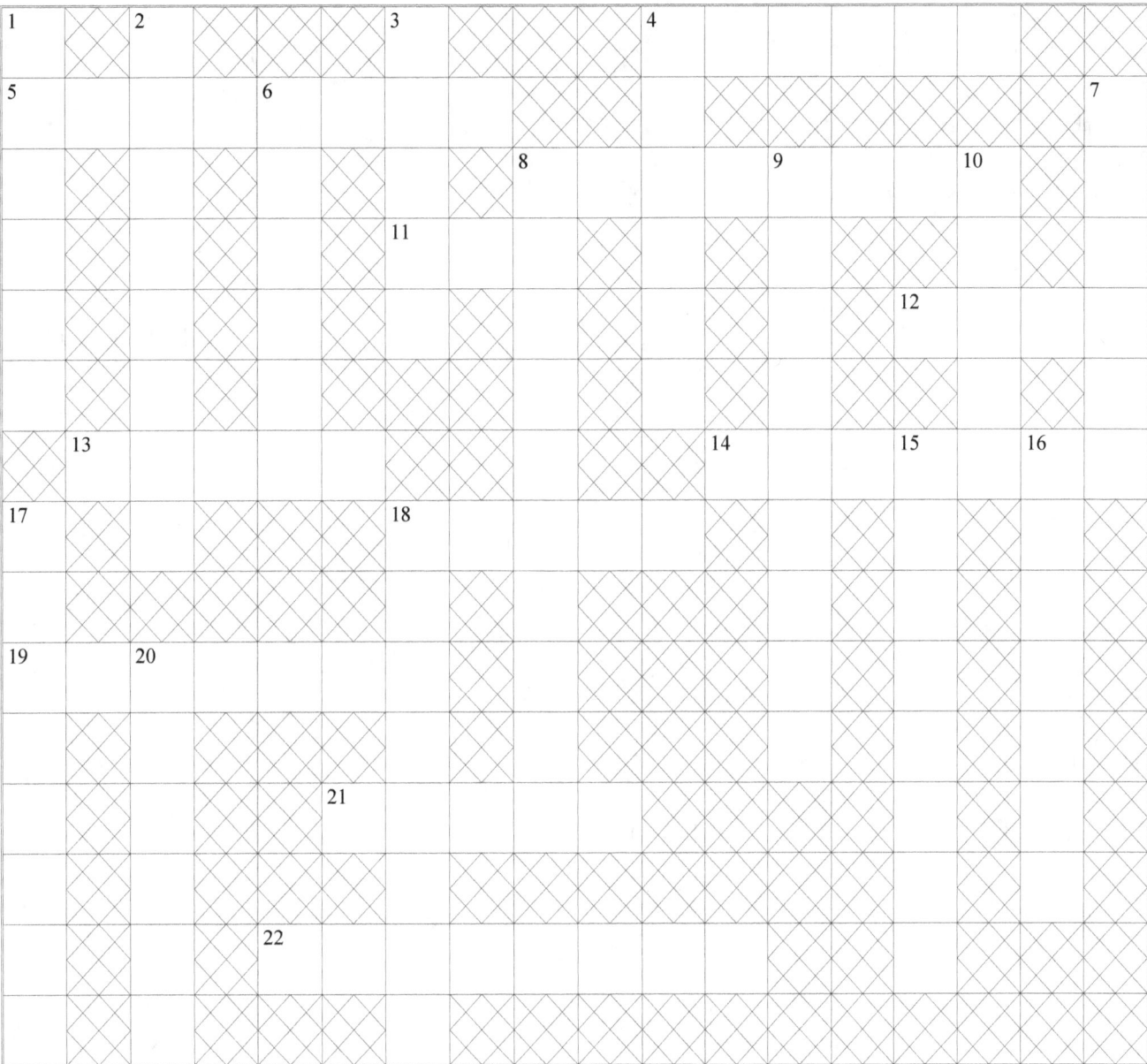

Across
- 4. Rapidly speak about unimportant matters
- 5. With warmth and sincerity
- 8. Showing ill will and a desire to hurt
- 11. Loud, harsh noise
- 12. The adult male of various deer
- 13. Something serving as proof of something else; a sign
- 14. Packages; wrapped-up items
- 18. Put up with; tolerate
- 19. Invigorating & stimulating tonic
- 21. Mythological creature composed of part man and part goat
- 22. Relied on with confidence

Down
- 1. High-pitched and piercing in tone or sound
- 2. Ornate tent
- 3. Open space in a forest
- 4. State of joyful exuberance or merriment
- 6. Something of little importance or value
- 7. Tree branches, especially large or main branches
- 8. In an irritable and short-tempered manner
- 9. Influenced by charms or spells
- 10. Gracefully slender; moving and blending with ease
- 15. Military operation or plan
- 16. Look with a sidelong glance with evil intent
- 17. Signaled or summoned, as by nodding or waving
- 18. Political partnership
- 20. Disorderly crowd of people

# VOCABULARY CROSSWORD ANSWER KEY - The Lion, The Witch, & The Wardrobe

|   |   |   |   |   |   |   |   |   |   |   |   |   |   |
|---|---|---|---|---|---|---|---|---|---|---|---|---|---|
| ¹S |   | ²P |   | ³G |   |   | ⁴G | I | B | B | E | R |   |
| ⁵H | E | A | R | ⁶T | I | L | Y |   |   |   |   |   | ⁷B |
| R |   | V |   | R |   |   | A |   | ⁸S | P | I | T | E | F | U | L | O |
| I |   | I |   | I |   | ¹¹D | I | N |   |   | E |   | ⁹F |   | ¹⁰L |   | U |
| L |   | L |   | L |   | E |   |   |   | T |   | C |   | ¹²S | T | A | G |
| L |   | I |   | L |   | F | E | A | T |   |   | H |   |   | H |   | H |
|   | ¹³T | O | K | E | N |   |   | P |   |   | ¹⁴P | A | ¹⁵R | C | ¹⁶E | L | ¹⁷S |
| ¹⁷B |   | N |   |   | ¹⁸A | B | I | D | E |   | A |   | A |   | M |   | E |
| E |   |   |   | L |   | S |   |   |   |   | T |   | M |   | E |   |   |
| ¹⁹C | ²⁰O | R | D | I | A | L |   | H |   |   | E |   | P |   | R |   |   |
| K |   | A |   | I |   |   |   | L |   |   | D |   | A |   | I |   |   |
| O |   | B |   | ²¹S | A | T | Y | R |   |   |   |   | I |   | N |   |   |
| N |   | B |   |   | N |   |   |   |   |   |   |   | G |   | G |   |   |
| E |   | L |   | ²²R | E | C | K | O | N | E | D |   | N |   |   |   |   |
| D |   | E |   |   | E |   |   |   |   |   |   |   |   |   |   |   |   |

Across
- 4. Rapidly speak about unimportant matters
- 5. With warmth and sincerity
- 8. Showing ill will and a desire to hurt
- 11. Loud, harsh noise
- 12. The adult male of various deer
- 13. Something serving as proof of something else; a sign
- 14. Packages; wrapped-up items
- 18. Put up with; tolerate
- 19. Invigorating & stimulating tonic
- 21. Mythological creature composed of part man and part goat
- 22. Relied on with confidence

Down
- 1. High-pitched and piercing in tone or sound
- 2. Ornate tent
- 3. Open space in a forest
- 4. State of joyful exuberance or merriment
- 6. Something of little importance or value
- 7. Tree branches, especially large or main branches
- 8. In an irritable and short-tempered manner
- 9. Influenced by charms or spells
- 10. Gracefully slender; moving and blending with ease
- 15. Military operation or plan
- 16. Look with a sidelong glance with evil intent
- 17. Signaled or summoned, as by nodding or waving
- 18. Political partnership
- 20. Disorderly crowd of people

# VOCABULARY MATCHING 1 - The Lion, The Witch, & The Wardrobe

___ 1. TRIFLE          A. Rapidly speak about unimportant matters
___ 2. HEARTILY        B. Decorative garlands of flowers or leaves
___ 3. BRISTLING       C. Disorderly crowd of people
___ 4. SATYR           D. Not to be relied on; not dependable or trustworthy; dangerous
___ 5. SLUICE          E. Showing ill will and a desire to hurt
___ 6. DRATTED         F. Something serving as proof of something else; a sign
___ 7. TREACHEROUS     G. High-pitched and piercing in tone or sound
___ 8. QUARRY          H. Something of little importance or value
___ 9. SPITEFUL        I. Invigorating & stimulating tonic
___10. RABBLE          J. Standing stiffly on end
___11. FESTOONS        K. Relied on with confidence
___12. STAG            L. Frustrating; cursed
___13. GLUTTONY        M. Packages; wrapped-up items
___14. VENTURED        N. With warmth and sincerity
___15. GIBBER          O. Open space in a forest
___16. RECKONED        P. A buzzing or whirring sound
___17. MELANCHOLY      Q. Sadness or depression of the spirits
___18. TOKEN           R. Took a risk; dared
___19. BURRING         S. Prey; a hunted animal
___20. LEERING         T. Kind of gate that controls the rate of water flow through a channel
___21. SHRILL          U. Excess in eating or drinking
___22. GLADE           V. Look with a sidelong glance with evil intent
___23. CORDIAL         W. The adult male of various deer
___24. SNAPPISHLY      X. Mythological creature composed of part man and part goat
___25. PARCELS         Y. In an irritable and short-tempered manner

# VOCABULARY MATCHING 1 ANSWER KEY - The Lion, The Witch, & The Wardrobe

| | | |
|---|---|---|
| H - 1. TRIFLE | A. | Rapidly speak about unimportant matters |
| N - 2. HEARTILY | B. | Decorative garlands of flowers or leaves |
| J - 3. BRISTLING | C. | Disorderly crowd of people |
| X - 4. SATYR | D. | Not to be relied on; not dependable or trustworthy; dangerous |
| T - 5. SLUICE | E. | Showing ill will and a desire to hurt |
| L - 6. DRATTED | F. | Something serving as proof of something else; a sign |
| D - 7. TREACHEROUS | G. | High-pitched and piercing in tone or sound |
| S - 8. QUARRY | H. | Something of little importance or value |
| E - 9. SPITEFUL | I. | Invigorating & stimulating tonic |
| C -10. RABBLE | J. | Standing stiffly on end |
| B -11. FESTOONS | K. | Relied on with confidence |
| W 12. STAG | L. | Frustrating; cursed |
| U -13. GLUTTONY | M. | Packages; wrapped-up items |
| R -14. VENTURED | N. | With warmth and sincerity |
| A -15. GIBBER | O. | Open space in a forest |
| K -16. RECKONED | P. | A buzzing or whirring sound |
| Q -17. MELANCHOLY | Q. | Sadness or depression of the spirits |
| F -18. TOKEN | R. | Took a risk; dared |
| P -19. BURRING | S. | Prey; a hunted animal |
| V -20. LEERING | T. | Kind of gate that controls the rate of water flow through a channel |
| G -21. SHRILL | U. | Excess in eating or drinking |
| O -22. GLADE | V. | Look with a sidelong glance with evil intent |
| I - 23. CORDIAL | W. | The adult male of various deer |
| Y -24. SNAPPISHLY | X. | Mythological creature composed of part man and part goat |
| M -25. PARCELS | Y. | In an irritable and short-tempered manner |

# VOCABULARY MATCHING 2 - The Lion, The Witch, & The Wardrobe

___ 1. SNAPPISHLY         A. Coming down and settling, as after flight
___ 2. MUFFLER            B. Frustrating; cursed
___ 3. DRATTED            C. Began again; continued after interruption
___ 4. CENTAUR            D. Associating with others in a brotherly way
___ 5. RABBLE             E. Put up with; tolerate
___ 6. FOREBODING         F. Standing stiffly on end
___ 7. FRATERNIZING       G. Military plan designed to deceive or surprise an enemy
___ 8. ABIDE              H. A disrespectful laugh
___ 9. SULKY              I. Look with a sidelong glance with evil intent
___ 10. SPRINGY           J. Elastic, soft, bouncy
___ 11. JOLLIFICATION     K. Verbal abuse; taunting
___ 12. BURRING           L. Open space in a forest
___ 13. HEARTILY          M. In an irritable and short-tempered manner
___ 14. SNIGGER           N. Disorderly crowd of people
___ 15. SLUICE            O. Relied on with confidence
___ 16. RECKONED          P. With warmth and sincerity
___ 17. STRATAGEM         Q. Kind of gate that controls the rate of water flow through a channel
___ 18. ALIGHTING         R. Pouting and withdrawn
___ 19. LITHE             S. Mythical being that is half man and half horse
___ 20. JEERING           T. Festivity; revelry
___ 21. DIN               U. Gracefully slender; moving and blending with ease
___ 22. GLADE             V. A buzzing or whirring sound
___ 23. LEERING           W. Heavy scarf worn around the neck for warmth
___ 24. RESUMED           X. Sense of impending evil or misfortune
___ 25. BRISTLING         Y. Loud, harsh noise

# VOCABULARY MATCHING 2 ANSWER KEY - The Lion, The Witch, & The Wardrobe

| | | |
|---|---|---|
| M - 1. | SNAPPISHLY | A. Coming down and settling, as after flight |
| W - 2. | MUFFLER | B. Frustrating; cursed |
| B - 3. | DRATTED | C. Began again; continued after interruption |
| S - 4. | CENTAUR | D. Associating with others in a brotherly way |
| N - 5. | RABBLE | E. Put up with; tolerate |
| X - 6. | FOREBODING | F. Standing stiffly on end |
| D - 7. | FRATERNIZING | G. Military plan designed to deceive or surprise an enemy |
| E - 8. | ABIDE | H. A disrespectful laugh |
| R - 9. | SULKY | I. Look with a sidelong glance with evil intent |
| J - 10. | SPRINGY | J. Elastic, soft, bouncy |
| T - 11. | JOLLIFICATION | K. Verbal abuse; taunting |
| V - 12. | BURRING | L. Open space in a forest |
| P - 13. | HEARTILY | M. In an irritable and short-tempered manner |
| H - 14. | SNIGGER | N. Disorderly crowd of people |
| Q - 15. | SLUICE | O. Relied on with confidence |
| O - 16. | RECKONED | P. With warmth and sincerity |
| G - 17. | STRATAGEM | Q. Kind of gate that controls the rate of water flow through a channel |
| A - 18. | ALIGHTING | R. Pouting and withdrawn |
| U - 19. | LITHE | S. Mythical being that is half man and half horse |
| K - 20. | JEERING | T. Festivity; revelry |
| Y - 21. | DIN | U. Gracefully slender; moving and blending with ease |
| L - 22. | GLADE | V. A buzzing or whirring sound |
| I - 23. | LEERING | W. Heavy scarf worn around the neck for warmth |
| C - 24. | RESUMED | X. Sense of impending evil or misfortune |
| F - 25. | BRISTLING | Y. Loud, harsh noise |

# VOCABULARY JUGGLE LETTERS 1 - The Lion, The Witch, & The Wardrobe

1. IELHT = 1. _____
   Gracefully slender; moving and blending with ease

2. NROHS = 2. _____
   Shaved

3. LERBAB = 3. _____
   Disorderly crowd of people

4. OHXA = 4. _____
   An act intended to deceive or trick

5. LIEALNCA = 5. _____
   Political partnership

6. IRLCOAD = 6. _____
   Invigorating & stimulating tonic

7. NTIQIEUVISI = 7. _____
   Inclined to investigate; eager for knowledge

8. IASPDOLS = 8. _____
   To allow one to use or be of service to another

9. ROCAPHM = 9. _____
   Compound made of bark and leaves, used to repel insects

10. LEVVTE = 10. _____
    Cover over with a soft, furry covering

11. AGTS = 11. _____
    The adult male of various deer

12. UYAQRR = 12. _____
    Prey; a hunted animal

13. GNSERGI = 13. _____
    A disrespectful laugh

14. NYLUGTOT = 14. _____
    Excess in eating or drinking

15. GHLNIIGTA = 15. _____
    Coming down and settling, as after flight

16. HEWT            =16. _____
                         Sharpen

17. SSEPIR          =17. _____
                         Structures that taper to a point at the top

18. ETRUACN         =18. _____
                         Mythical being that is half man and half horse

19. ENOEDCNRU       =19. _____
                         Given up, especially by formal announcement

20. RETRUT          =20. _____
                         Small tower extending above a building

21. TONIOLIFJCALI   =21. _____
                         Festivity; revelry

22. RBBGEI          =22. _____
                         Rapidly speak about unimportant matters

23. ILESVERPU       =23. _____
                         Offensive or disgusting

24. STYAELB         =24. _____
                         Very disagreeable; unpleasant

25. CDYOE           =25. _____
                         Something used to lure victims into danger

26. KYUSL           =26. _____
                         Pouting and withdrawn

27. LUNLLGI         =27. _____
                         Soothing; calming; causing to sleep or rest

28. ERNELIG         =28. _____
                         Look with a sidelong glance with evil intent

29. GSEELD          =29. _____
                         Vehicle mounted on runners, drawn by work animals across ice

30. CEODNERK        =30. _____
                         Relied on with confidence

31. MNGCAAIP        =31. _____
                         Military operation or plan

32. MOLNES =32. _____
Deeply earnest, serious, and sober

33. COYRPPEH =33. _____
Prediction of the future

34. NITAIONTANC =34. _____
Words believed to have a magical effect; a spell

35. ULBRNUMA =35. _____
Kind of tree with clusters of yellow flowers

36. GOIPIOSURD =36. _____
Impressively great in size or force

VOCABULARY JUGGLE LETTERS 1 ANSWER KEY - The Lion, The Witch, & The Wardrobe

1. IELHT = 1. LITHE
   Gracefully slender; moving and blending with ease

2. NROHS = 2. SHORN
   Shaved

3. LERBAB = 3. RABBLE
   Disorderly crowd of people

4. OHXA = 4. HOAX
   An act intended to deceive or trick

5. LIEALNCA = 5. ALLIANCE
   Political partnership

6. IRLCOAD = 6. CORDIAL
   Invigorating & stimulating tonic

7. NTIQIEUVISI = 7. INQUISITIVE
   Inclined to investigate; eager for knowledge

8. IASPDOLS = 8. DISPOSAL
   To allow one to use or be of service to another

9. ROCAPHM = 9. CAMPHOR
   Compound made of bark and leaves, used to repel insects

10. LEVVTE = 10. VELVET
    Cover over with a soft, furry covering

11. AGTS = 11. STAG
    The adult male of various deer

12. UYAQRR = 12. QUARRY
    Prey; a hunted animal

13. GNSERGI = 13. SNIGGER
    A disrespectful laugh

14. NYLUGTOT = 14. GLUTTONY
    Excess in eating or drinking

15. GHLNIIGTA = 15. ALIGHTING
    Coming down and settling, as after flight

16. HEWT =16. WHET
Sharpen

17. SSEPIR =17. SPIRES
Structures that taper to a point at the top

18. ETRUACN =18. CENTAUR
Mythical being that is half man and half horse

19. ENOEDCNRU =19. RENOUNCED
Given up, especially by formal announcement

20. RETRUT =20. TURRET
Small tower extending above a building

21. TONIOLIFJCALI =21. JOLLIFICATION
Festivity; revelry

22. RBBGEI =22. GIBBER
Rapidly speak about unimportant matters

23. ILESVERPU =23. REPULSIVE
Offensive or disgusting

24. STYAELB =24. BEASTLY
Very disagreeable; unpleasant

25. CDYOE =25. DECOY
Something used to lure victims into danger

26. KYUSL =26. SULKY
Pouting and withdrawn

27. LUNLLGI =27. LULLING
Soothing; calming; causing to sleep or rest

28. ERNELIG =28. LEERING
Look with a sidelong glance with evil intent

29. GSEELD =29. SLEDGE
Vehicle mounted on runners, drawn by work animals across ice

30. CEODNERK =30. RECKONED
Relied on with confidence

31. MNGCAAIP =31. CAMPAIGN
Military operation or plan

32. MOLNES =32. SOLEMN
Deeply earnest, serious, and sober

33. COYRPPEH =33. PROPHECY
Prediction of the future

34. NITAIONTANC =34. INCANTATION
Words believed to have a magical effect; a spell

35. ULBRNUMA =35. LABURNUM
Kind of tree with clusters of yellow flowers

36. GOIPIOSURD =36. PRODIGIOUS
Impressively great in size or force

# VOCABULARY JUGGLE LETTERS 2 - The Lion, The Witch, & The Wardrobe

1. CSIELU = 1. _____
   Kind of gate that controls the rate of water flow through a channel

2. RNGEEJI = 2. _____
   Verbal abuse; taunting

3. URSDEEM = 3. _____
   Began again; continued after interruption

4. OGDNREFBOI = 4. _____
   Sense of impending evil or misfortune

5. EAMTLN = 5. _____
   Loose, sleeveless coat worn over outer garments; cloak

6. FFERLUM = 6. _____
   Heavy scarf worn around the neck for warmth

7. IPNGYSR = 7. _____
   Elastic, soft, bouncy

8. LISHRL = 8. _____
   High-pitched and piercing in tone or sound

9. RESRTEAHUCO = 9. _____
   Not to be relied on; not dependable or trustworthy; dangerous

10. USFLIETP =10. _____
    Showing ill will and a desire to hurt

11. EMSRANTN =11. _____
    Left-overs

12. TEARDDT =12. _____
    Frustrating; cursed

13. NCDAHNETE =13. _____
    Influenced by charms or spells

14. ARYRODNI =14. _____
    Of no exceptional ability

15. EBNA =15. _____
    Cause of harm, ruin, or death

16. MEGTSAATR    =16. _____
                 Military plan designed to deceive or surprise an enemy

17. KNOTE        =17. _____
                 Something serving as proof of something else; a sign

18. LSPRACE      =18. _____
                 Packages; wrapped-up items

19. GAELD        =19. _____
                 Open space in a forest

20. IEHYALTR     =20. _____
                 With warmth and sincerity

21. NEVUREDT     =21. _____
                 Took a risk; dared

22. EDPRTOO      =22. _____
                 Moved as a group

23. DKCONEEB     =23. _____
                 Signaled or summoned, as by nodding or waving

24. LRTFIE       =24. _____
                 Something of little importance or value

25. RTDHECWE     =25. _____
                 Of a poor or mean character

26. EBADI        =26. _____
                 Put up with; tolerate

27. LLMNCEYAHO   =27. _____
                 Sadness or depression of the spirits

28. GOHUSB       =28. _____
                 Tree branches, especially large or main branches

29. IRZGFTNREAIN =29. _____
                 Associating with others in a brotherly way

30. RBOWEDRA     =30. _____
                 Tall cabinet or closet built to hold clothes

31. AYRST        =31. _____
                 Mythological creature composed of part man and part goat

32. HPSILPSYAN =32. _____
In an irritable and short-tempered manner

33. GIRRBNU =33. _____
A buzzing or whirring sound

34. IEVMNR =34. _____
Pests; people considered hateful or highly offensive

35. LSAEDPR =35. _____
British word for one who travels about selling wares

36. NDI =36. _____
Loud, harsh noise

VOCABULARY JUGGLE LETTERS 2 ANSWER KEY - The Lion, The Witch, & The Wardrobe

1. CSIELU = 1. SLUICE
Kind of gate that controls the rate of water flow through a channel

2. RNGEEJI = 2. JEERING
Verbal abuse; taunting

3. URSDEEM = 3. RESUMED
Began again; continued after interruption

4. OGDNREFBOI = 4. FOREBODING
Sense of impending evil or misfortune

5. EAMTLN = 5. MANTLE
Loose, sleeveless coat worn over outer garments; cloak

6. FFERLUM = 6. MUFFLER
Heavy scarf worn around the neck for warmth

7. IPNGYSR = 7. SPRINGY
Elastic, soft, bouncy

8. LISHRL = 8. SHRILL
High-pitched and piercing in tone or sound

9. RESRTEAHUCO = 9. TREACHEROUS
Not to be relied on; not dependable or trustworthy; dangerous

10. USFLIETP =10. SPITEFUL
Showing ill will and a desire to hurt

11. EMSRANTN =11. REMNANTS
Left-overs

12. TEARDDT =12. DRATTED
Frustrating; cursed

13. NCDAHNETE =13. ENCHANTED
Influenced by charms or spells

14. ARYRODNI =14. ORDINARY
Of no exceptional ability

15. EBNA =15. BANE
Cause of harm, ruin, or death

16. MEGTSAATR =16. STRATAGEM

Military plan designed to deceive or surprise an enemy

17. KNOTE =17. TOKEN

Something serving as proof of something else; a sign

18. LSPRACE =18. PARCELS

Packages; wrapped-up items

19. GAELD =19. GLADE

Open space in a forest

20. IEHYALTR =20. HEARTILY

With warmth and sincerity

21. NEVUREDT =21. VENTURED

Took a risk; dared

22. EDPRTOO =22. TROOPED

Moved as a group

23. DKCONEEB =23. BECKONED

Signaled or summoned, as by nodding or waving

24. LRTFIE =24. TRIFLE

Something of little importance or value

25. RTDHECWE =25. WRETCHED

Of a poor or mean character

26. EBADI =26. ABIDE

Put up with; tolerate

27. LLMNCEYAHO =27. MELANCHOLY

Sadness or depression of the spirits

28. GOHUSB =28. BOUGHS

Tree branches, especially large or main branches

29. IRZGFTNREAIN =29. FRATERNIZING

Associating with others in a brotherly way

30. RBOWEDRA =30. WARDROBE

Tall cabinet or closet built to hold clothes

31. AYRST =31. SATYR

Mythological creature composed of part man and part goat

32. HPSILPSYAN = 32. SNAPPISHLY

In an irritable and short-tempered manner

33. GIRRBNU = 33. BURRING

A buzzing or whirring sound

34. IEVMNR = 34. VERMIN

Pests; people considered hateful or highly offensive

35. LSAEDPR = 35. PEDLARS

British word for one who travels about selling wares

36. NDI = 36. DIN

Loud, harsh noise

www.ingramcontent.com/pod-product-compliance
Lightning Source LLC
Chambersburg PA
CBHW051406070526
44584CB00023B/3318